D0403341

GLOBAL ECONOMIC IMBALANCES

SPECIAL REPORTS 4

GLOBAL ECONOMIC IMBALANCES

Edited by
C. Fred Bergsten

INSTITUTE FOR INTERNATIONAL ECONOMICS
Washington, DC
December 1985

Dr. C. Fred Bergsten is Director of the Institute for International Economics. He was formerly Assistant Secretary of the Treasury for International Affairs; Assistant for International Economic Affairs to the National Security Council; and a Senior Fellow at the Carnegie Endowment for International Peace, The Brookings Institution, and the Council on Foreign Relations.

INSTITUTE FOR INTERNATIONAL ECONOMICS
C. Fred Bergsten, *Director*
Kathleen A. Lynch, *Director of Publications*
Michelle K. Smith, *Editorial Assistant*
Stephen Kraft, *Designer*

The Institute for International Economics was created and is principally funded by the German Marshall Fund of the United States.

The views expressed in this publication are those of the authors. This publication is part of the overall program of the Institute, as endorsed by its Board of Directors, but does not necessarily reflect the views of the individual members of the Board or the Advisory Committee.

Copyright © December 1985 Institute for International Economics. All rights reserved. No part of this book may be reproduced or utilized in any form or by any means, electronic or mechanical, including photocopying, recording, or by information storage or retrieval system, without written permission from the Institute.

Library of Congress Cataloging in Publication Data
Main entry under title:

Global Economic Imbalances.

Papers were presented at a conference held in Washington, DC, on September 21–23, 1984.
1. Economic policy—Congresses. 2. Commerce—Congresses. 3. Debts, External—Congresses.
I. Bergsten, C. Fred. 1941– , II. Institute for International Economics (U.S.)
HD73.I43   330.9′048   85–8279
ISBN 0–88132–038–2

Contents

INSTITUTE FOR INTERNATIONAL ECONOMICS
11 Dupont Circle, NW, Washington, DC 20036
(202) 328-0583 Telex: 248329 CEIP

C. Fred Bergsten, *Director*

BOARD OF DIRECTORS

Peter G. Peterson, *Chairman*

Raymond Barre
W. Michael Blumenthal
Douglas A. Fraser
Alan Greenspan
Abdlatif Y. al-Hamad
Reginald H. Jones
Frank E. Loy
Donald F. McHenry
Saburo Okita
I. G. Patel
Karl Otto Pohl
David Rockefeller
Donna E. Shalala
Mario Henrique Simonsen
Anthony M. Solomon
Dennis Weatherstone
Andrew Young

Ex officio
C. Fred Bergsten
Richard N. Cooper

Honorary Directors
George P. Shultz
John N. Turner

ADVISORY COMMITTEE

Richard N. Cooper, *Chairman*

Robert Baldwin
Lester R. Brown
Rimmer de Vries
Rudiger Dornbusch
Robert J. Flanagan
Isaiah Frank
Jacob A. Frenkel
Herbert Giersch
Gottfried Haberler
Mahbub ul Haq
Arnold C. Harberger
Dale E. Hathaway
Nurul Islam
Peter B. Kenen
Lawrence R. Klein
Ryutaro Komiya
Lawrence B. Krause
Roger M. Kubarych
Assar Lindbeck
Harald B. Malmgren
Richard R. Nelson
Joseph S. Nye, Jr.
Rudolph A. Oswald
Jacques J. Polak
Ernest Stern
Philip K. Verleger, Jr.
Henry C. Wallich
Marina v.N. Whitman
Alan Wm. Wolff

Preface

In September 1984, the Institute held a conference in Washington which brought together for the first time, to our knowledge, most of the research institutions throughout the world which are conducting significant studies of international economic issues. As indicated in more detail in my introduction to the volume, the purposes were to discuss some of the central issues facing the world economy; to consider the research programs of the various centers; and to expand the opportunity for exchanges among them.

This volume presents the papers prepared for the conference, summaries of the discussion of each, the views expressed by a panel composed to draw policy conclusions from the papers and these discussions, and a synopsis of the research agendas submitted by a number of the participating institutions.

Fifty institutions from twenty-five countries and five international economic organizations attended the conference. As a result of its discussions, they decided to hold such sessions regularly in the future and to institutionalize the exchange of information on their respective agendas. The next meeting will take place at the Institute in September 1986.

The idea of instituting periodic conferences to bring together the family of research centers working on international economics was inspired to a considerable degree by the annual meetings held by the International Institute for Strategic Studies in London for the community of researchers on international security issues. Extensive consultations were held in late 1983 and early 1984 with the directors of a number of leading institutes in all parts of the world to consider the idea from which emerged widespread support for proceeding on an experimental basis. The Ford Foundation made the effort possible and was particularly instrumental in enabling representatives from a number of institutions in developing countries to attend the conference.

The conference was organized primarily by Stephen Marris, a Senior Fellow at the Institute, and myself. Miguel A. Kiguel, then a Research Associate at the Institute, assisted in analyzing and summarizing the research agendas submitted by thirty of the participating institutions. Carol Fox, Executive Assistant to the Director, handled all administrative arrangements.

The Institute for International Economics is a private nonprofit research institution for the study and discussion of international economic policy. Its purpose is to analyze important issues in that area and to develop and communicate practical new approaches for dealing with them.

The Institute was created in November 1981 through a generous commitment of funds from the German Marshall Fund of the United States. Support is being received from other private foundations and corporations, and the Institute is now broadening and diversifying its financial base.

The Board of Directors bears overall responsibility for the Institute and gives general guidance and approval to its research program— including identification of topics that are likely to become important to international economic policymakers over the medium run (generally, one to three years) and which thus should be addressed by the Institute. The Director of the Institute, working closely with the staff and outside Advisory Committee, is responsible for the development of particular projects and makes the final decision to publish an individual study. The Institute is completely nonpartisan.

The Institute hopes that its studies and other activities will contribute to building a stronger foundation for international economic policy around the world. Comments as to how it can best do so are invited from readers of these publications.

C. FRED BERGSTEN
Director
December 1985

1 Introduction

The Institute for International Economics hosted a conference for the directors or other senior representatives of fifty research institutions from twenty-five countries and five international economic organizations in Washington on September 21–23, 1984. A few individuals, also engaged in significant research on international economic issues, participated as well. The Institute attempted to bring together all centers involved in such research, for the first time, for three purposes:

- to discuss some of the central intellectual and policy issues confronting the world economy
- to consider whether the research agendas being pursued by the centers and individuals represented met the most salient intellectual and policy needs
- to enable the institutions engaged in international economic research to become better acquainted with each other, in the hope of fostering more effective interchange and cooperation among them—and thus a greater contribution to knowledge and policy formulation in the future.

The substantive focus of the conference was deliberately broad, to encompass priority concerns of both industrial and developing countries. "Global Economic Imbalances" was defined to include three types of problems: shortcomings and inconsistencies in national macroeconomic policies, structural weaknesses and supply-side concerns, and trade policy issues (including those related to "industrial policies"). The author of each of the five main papers was asked to address this nexus of problems from his own geographical vantage point, and commentators from different regions were selected to provide a variety of perspectives. In keeping with the second focus of the meeting, on research agendas, each author was also asked to suggest topics emerging from his analysis that needed further study. The comments of the discussants are summarized after each paper. A separate chapter summarizes the general discussion on the policy implications of the individual presentations and sessions.

Martin S. Feldstein launched the conference with a presentation on the recent economic performance and policies of the United States, emphasizing their effects on the rest of the world. Richard G. Lipsey began the discussion, speaking from the viewpoint of Canada, and Luigi Spaventa introduced a European perspective. Armin Gutowski of Germany chaired the panel. After the conclusion of this session, over lunch, the conferees were offered another American perspective—this time centered on trade policy—by Ambassador William E. Brock, the United States Trade Representative.

The second session of the conference focused on the other industrial countries, with papers by Edmond Malinvaud of France and Masaru Yoshitomi of Japan. The initial commentators were Herbert Giersch of Germany, presenting an alternative view of the European outlook, and Lawrence B. Krause with an American view of Japanese developments. Paul W. McCracken of the United States chaired the discussion.

The third segment of the conference turned to the vantage point of the developing countries. Papers were presented by Mario Henrique Simonsen of Brazil, an advanced developing country, and Deepak Lal of India, one of the poorer nations. Commentary was initially offered by Bela Balassa of the United States and Amir H. Jamal of Tanzania, and Jagdish N. Bhagwati of the United States and India chaired the panel.

The final substantive discussion of the conference was launched by a panel selected to discuss the policy implications of the foregoing exchanges, again from a series of different national perspectives. In that vein an American view was offered by Richard N. Cooper, a Japanese appraisal by Saburo Okita, a European approach by Stephen Marris, and a presentation focused on the developing countries by I. G. Patel. An effort was made to draw inferences for each region although, in the event, most comments addressed the US policy mix and its external implications, and the structural and cyclical problems currently confronting Europe.

Questions of research, in both substantive and procedural terms, were taken up on the last day. The objective was to enable the institutions represented to learn more about the nature of their colleagues' work programs, in an effort to promote more extensive interchange in a way that would permit researchers in this field to build more effectively on projects underway in other centers. In preparation for this part of the meeting, the Institute had asked participating institutions to submit descriptions of their own research programs for inclusion in a summary which, along with the substantive papers, was distributed in advance and is included as appendix C in this volume.

The discussion of research agendas was launched with presentations by Anne O. Krueger of the United States (and the World Bank) and, from a political economy perspective, Thierry de Montbrial of France. Initial comments were offered by William H. Branson of the United States and Ahn Seung-Chul of Korea, with the session chaired by C. Fred Bergsten.

The conference closed with a luncheon for the directors of participating institutions given by the Director of the Institute. Its purpose was to discuss the array of possibilities for intensifying and systematizing collaboration among the institutions engaged in significant research on international economic issues, most of which were represented at the meeting. Numerous ideas were suggested, and a good deal of enthusiasm was expressed for pursuing more active interchange within the group.

Virtually all participants indicated a desire to engage in regularly scheduled conferences of the type launched here, so that the institutes working on international economic issues could maintain active discussions on both substantive topics and their respective research agendas. Some directors preferred annual sessions while others thought biennial conferences would be adequate. Some suggested a greater focus on research agendas and priorities; others voiced a desire to maintain the mix of substance and research agendas embodied in this first exercise; still others would opt for almost exclusive attention to substance, perhaps with more narrowly defined topics to encourage greater depth of discussion. There were also proposals to hold periodic "subconferences" to discuss research on particular aspects of international economics, such as trade or international monetary affairs, and to create a permanent association of institutions engaged in international economic research.

To date, three decisions have been made in light of these exchanges: to continue on a regular basis the series of conferences of research institutes begun in September 1984, to meet biennially, and for the Institute to host the next conference in Washington in September 1986. (The conference would again be linked to the Annual Meetings of the International Monetary Fund and World Bank, as in 1984, which met with widespread approval.) Past and future participants in the process will consult on the topics to be discussed and the mix of items for the agenda.

A second area of nearly total consensus was on the need for systematic, ongoing exchanges of information among the research institutes concerning their respective programs and priorities. The compilation of agendas prepared for this conference was viewed as a useful model of what needed to be done in order to improve the dissemination of knowledge about work in progress. Several participants hoped that such information could be more detailed and could be provided early in the research process. At the suggestion of a number of participants, the Institute has decided to undertake such an effort and is now working on its modalities.

All participants were asked to reflect further on the outcome of the conference and to convey additional thoughts both on the session itself and on possibilities for future cooperation. A large number took the opportunity to do so, and the process of continuing consultation seems to be well underway.

This volume comprises the papers presented to this first meeting of institutions engaged in research on international economic issues, summaries of the comments on them by formal discussants and other conference participants, and the compilation of research agendas prepared for the meeting. It is hoped this book will be the first of a series emanating from an ongoing set of conferences of this particular family of research centers.

2 The View from North America

Martin S. Feldstein

The topic that I have been assigned—the imbalances in the US economy and their impact abroad—is a formidable task given the expertise that is assembled here. The basic nature of the problem is well known to you, but I would like to give you my interpretation of those two imbalances:

- the domestic imbalances—the deficits in the federal budget
- the international imbalances—our trade deficit and its mirror image, the capital account imbalance

I also want to discuss the link between the domestic and international imbalances—the dollar.

I shall begin by reviewing the situation in the United States with respect to the government deficit and its domestic impact. My basic point is that although the 1982–83 deficits were not on balance a problem for the American economy, probably doing more good than harm, the deficits that we face now and into the future will do substantial damage.

After exploring the domestic impact of this imbalance, I shall discuss the rise in the dollar over the last four years, the role of the budget deficit in that rise, and the impact of the higher dollar. The most obvious consequence of the stronger dollar, as seen from this side of the ocean, is the damage to US industry. Less obvious is that the increase in the dollar has served as a useful safety valve that has prevented an even higher real interest rate in the United States in response to the large budget deficit. In other words, the rise in the dollar is a healthy market response to a serious underlying problem. Finally, I shall discuss very briefly my own speculations about the effect of the US deficit on Europe and on the debtor countries in the developing world.

Let me begin with the budget deficit in the United States. The deficit for fiscal year 1984 is going to be about $170 billion. Realistic projections indicate that, by the end of the decade, if there is no further legislative action, the deficit will increase to about $250 billion. Had the legislative action known as the downpayment package not occurred in the summer of 1984, the deficit by the end of the decade would have been over $300 billion.

Seen in terms of a constant unemployment rate of 6.5 percent, the structural deficit rose from about $100 billion in 1983 to $140 billion in 1984. That is, $140 billion of $170 billion of the 1984 deficit was structural. Without legislative action this portion will continue to rise until, by the end of the decade, essentially the entire $250 billion budget deficit will be structural.

The impact of such deficits will be substantial. The clearest effect is the increase in the US national debt—about $1,000 billion over the next five years—and its consequences. To put that number in perspective, the gross national product at the end of the decade is projected at $5.5 trillion. The increase in the national debt would be nearly 20 percent of GNP. The resulting interest costs, assuming no change in current interest levels (about 12 percent), would be $120 billion a year. Such costs would be cause for a tax increase of $120 billion a year, 20 percent of the current projected levels of personal and corporate income tax revenue. The distortions arising from those higher tax rates are part of the permanent costs of running budget deficits of the magnitude currently projected.

The second long-term cumulative effect of high deficits is on capital accumulation. Excluding the savings of state and local governments, net nonfederal saving is less than 8 percent of GNP. The projected deficits mean that the government is absorbing somewhat more than half of all the net savings generated domestically in the United States, leaving net investments of less than 4 percent of GNP except for the capital inflow. Even with that capital inflow, the net effect is clearly slower growth and lower future productivity.

What about the short-run effects of persistent high budget deficits? I have stated that the 1982–83 deficits actually helped the recovery by adding to consumer demand directly and therefore to overall GNP. Nevertheless, I would not exaggerate the importance of those deficits in stimulating the recovery. Future research will have to sort out how much of the strong recovery in the last two years was due to fiscal stimulus and how much to changes in monetary conditions.

Deficits now and in the future seem to have moved from being a positive factor to being a harmful one for the economy because they are creating serious imbalances in the structure of demand—imbalances that become more important as full employment nears. The most obvious of those imbalances has been the trade deficit—an unprecedented merchandise trade gap running at about 3 percent of GNP.

In addition, capital accumulation has been lower than it would have been otherwise. The recent significant upturn in spending on plant and equipment followed a period of very low investment spending. We actually had negative net investment at the end of 1982 and the beginning of 1983. So, even with the sharp upturn, net investment is still at the low end of recent average performance.

Moreover, we are beginning to see a slowdown in some capital spending. Housing starts, which had until recently been kept up by a backlog, have begun to drop substantially and are down to about 1.5 million units annually.

From this consideration of the purely domestic impact of the budget deficit, let me turn to the international imbalances. Since 1980 the dollar has gone up by a remarkable 60 percent in real terms calculated on a multilateral trade-weighted basis. The deficit is an important reason, but not the only reason.

A more inclusive explanation is that US investments are now more attractive, compared with foreign investments, than they were a few years ago; they have a relatively higher expected return and are perceived to be much less risky. The reasons for that higher return and lower risk are threefold: changes in monetary policy, changes in tax policy, and changes in the budget deficit.

US monetary policy tightened in 1979, temporarily pushing up real interest rates from a purely monetary point of view. But of more sustained importance has been the shift in the perceived risk of inflation in the United States that resulted from the shift in Federal Reserve policy. The Fed's tenacity—the credibility that it has developed—has given the correct impression that a sound monetary policy will continue to be pursued. That has made investment in US securities lower risk than in the pre-1979 period.

The second factor enhancing the attractiveness of US securities has been the change in US tax policy. In 1981 a major change in tax rules increased after-tax rates of return. Depreciation has been cut and effective tax rates reduced. In addition, the fall in inflation has, in itself, reduced effective tax rates because of the way inflation reduces the present value of depreciation. This combination of lower inflation rates and formal changes in tax rules has significantly increased after-tax rates of return and therefore the interest rates that firms are able and willing to pay for debt and equity capital. That in turn reinforces the pretax differences in profitability that may well have widened between the United States and Europe in the past half decade or so.

In addition to these changes in monetary and tax policy, I would emphasize the substantial increase in the government deficit. Because those deficits are absorbing about half of all net savings, they inevitably push up interest rates. This shrinks private demand for funds, and supplements that demand for funds with an inflow of capital from abroad.

It is no paradox that a large actual and projected budget deficit in this country should be the source of the strengthening of the dollar. The fundamental difference in monetary policies explains the seeming paradox between the US experience and the foreign experience, where a large budget deficit has often led to a deterioration in the exchange rate. In other countries large budget deficits have very frequently been accompanied by a monetization of the resulting increase in debt, either as an implicit policy decision or because the domestic capital markets were not well enough developed to absorb additional government debt. The United States, however, has had a continued sound monetary policy and an expectation that it will remain sound. That expectation, combined with large budget deficits, has allowed real interest rates to attract funds from the rest of the world.

Let me briefly address the impact of the strong dollar on the US economy. Three distinct effects should be noted. First, the dollar has helped to slow the rate of inflation. The consumer price index (CPI) is probably 5 percentage points lower than it would have been if the dollar had not increased as it did over the past four years. The current inflation rate is probably from 1 percentage point to 1½ percentage points below where it would have been if the dollar had not risen over the last 18 to 24 months.

Second, and the one most obvious to the public, is the effect of the strong dollar on the US trade deficit. From the late 1970s to 1980, the United States had a merchandise trade deficit of about $25 billion a year. By 1983 that had jumped to $60 billion and in 1984 it ran well over $100 billion. It is obviously doing quite substantial damage to particular firms and industries that are or used to be in the export business or that compete with imports from abroad.

Moreover, the strong dollar is having longer term effects as American firms look abroad for sources of inputs that were previously obtained in the United States. They look abroad to locate whole new manufacturing facilities to take advantage of the changes in the exchange rate. In addition, the very substantial damage that the strong dollar is doing to particular industries is encouraging protectionism in the United States. The current administration's basic instincts are for free trade, but it is operating in an environment that is unusually hostile to free trade.

The third effect receives the least attention and it is the one I want to emphasize: the strong dollar's impact on the capital inflow. The United States was a capital exporter for almost the entire postwar period; it was still running a surplus in the capital account in 1980 and 1981 despite its merchandise trade deficit of about $25 billion. But in 1982 that switched; the current account deficit was $9 billion; in 1983, $43 billion; and recently over $100 billion. The United States has become a dramatic importer of capital; $100 billion is nearly 3 percent of GNP. It is more than half of the budget deficit and about two-thirds of the structural budget deficit. It represents a 50 percent increase in the net funds available for investment in the United States. This can have a very dramatic effect on US capital markets, keeping interest rates lower and equity prices higher than they otherwise would be. Of course, this is just a temporary effect; it is not sustainable.

Capital imports have been a useful safety valve for the American economy, allowing it to make the best of the bad problem of budget deficits. The dollar's rise is a healthy, normal market response to that bad problem. It spreads the pain around; it avoids the problems that would come from concentrating the crowding out solely on the capital goods and capital formation part of the US economy. It would therefore have been inappropriate to try to prevent this increase in the dollar by intervention or by capital controls even if those might have worked.

Let me conclude by looking at the impact of these US imbalances on the economies of Europe and on the less developed debtor countries. With respect to Europe, there are clearly both pluses and minuses of the recent US imbalances. To start with the positive effects, the strong US recovery and the strong dollar have increased European exports to the rest of the world, not only to the United States but to the third markets in which the United States competes, and have reduced European and third-country imports from the United States. A second favorable effect: the improved trade balances spurred recovery in Europe and permitted several European countries to pursue more expansionary domestic policies than they might otherwise have been able to do.

But there have been negative effects as well. With the declining exchange rate, these European countries experienced increasing inflationary pressures. To prevent or to limit the actual increase in inflation, they frequently pursued contractionary monetary and fiscal policies.

Which effect on the European recovery was stronger is still an unanswered question. My own conjecture is that without the increase in the US deficit and without the strong dollar, the recovery in Europe would have been weaker than it has been. But I would like to see careful research on that.

A second adverse effect in Europe in response to the US imbalance has been a change in the composition of GNP in European countries. The capital outflow from Europe to the United States has meant more investment in the United States and less in Europe than there otherwise would have been. I would argue that the US deficit leads to a better global allocation of resources than would have occurred had the United States simply bottled up the two separate capital markets and not allowed imbalances in trade and the capital flow—imbalances should not be read in this context as a bad word. Of course individual countries could have tried to offset this tendency for investment to fall at home. Although they might not have been able to influence the real interest rate faced by their domestic capital market, they could have changed their domestic fiscal incentives to encourage investment at home and some countries did.

Finally, turning to the impact of the US imbalances on the LDC debtor countries, again there are pluses and minuses. The higher real interest rates that resulted from the deficit were clearly adverse for these countries. The real interest rate increased about 3 percent over this period. In Brazil's case that represents a rise of $3 billion a year in the increased real cost of servicing its international debt—more than 10 percent of its gross exports. So it puts an extra strain on the debtor countries in their attempts to service their debt and forces them to restrict their imports. That restriction in turn has had adverse consequences for their domestic rate of economic growth.

A second effect of US policies, the higher dollar, has had a more ambiguous impact on the debtor countries. The direct effect of the higher dollar is to increase the real value of the debt and that is unequivocally an additional burden to the debtor countries. When I say it increased the real value of the debt, what I have in mind is that only a fraction of the exports of those countries are sold to the United States; the others are sold to nondollar countries and, therefore, for a given physical volume of exports, the rise in the dollar raises the ratio of the value of the debt to the value of the exports.

The higher dollar also has a favorable effect, hence the ambiguity. It increases exports and decreases imports. Latin America does about 40 percent of its trade with the United States, and virtually all of the trade improvement of Latin America in the last few years has been due to the United States and Japan. The stronger dollar has, in that sense, helped these countries improve their trade and current account balances.

The net impact is uncertain and again this seems to be an area that needs additional research. The answer may well differ from country to country. I look forward to hearing your comments.

Chapter 2 Discussion

Richard G. Lipsey and Luigi Spaventa were the formal discussants of Professor Feldstein's presentation. Lipsey had little criticism for Feldstein, sharing his desire to see a decline in the US budget deficit. He noted that the Canadian dollar was also at "very high" levels, for the same reasons as the American dollar, despite the fact that Canada had "the highest unit labor costs in the world" and was experiencing "the weakest recovery in its history"—which make reductions in its own budget deficit extremely difficult to achieve.

Lipsey noted that the US situation presented an acute dilemma for Canada. Continuing American budget deficits would perpetuate high interest rates and bring on a new recession. But a sharp decline in the dollar would accelerate inflation and Canada's wage-price pressures, which were already substantial. He thought that Canada's only unilateral option was to try to change its policy mix on its own, but concluded it was "unclear" whether Canada could "go it alone."

Spaventa thought that the US situation was positive for Europe, on balance, although negative side effects existed as well. He thought there was excessive European criticism of the United States, "whatever happens there," and that such complaints concealed the need for action by Europe itself.

Spaventa believed that Feldstein was too optimistic in thinking that the growth in the US current account deficit relieved European countries—at least the larger ones—from external constraints. In particular, he opposed recent US efforts to overtly "solicit" more capital inflows. Europe's best response, however, was to keep capital at home by promoting rapid economic growth and thus reducing the imbalance between domestic savings and investment.

A number of speakers took the view that the US situation, as described by Feldstein, was on balance positive for the United States itself or for the rest of the world, or both.

Herbert Giersch argued that the strong dollar was promoting the inevitable structural adjustment of the US economy, as caused by increasing competition from newly industrializing countries (although C. Fred Bergsten noted that some of the adjustment, such as foreign investment by American firms, was an uneconomic response to incorrect price signals). In addition, the US deficits were helping to resolve the LDC debt crisis; Giersch contrasted current US behavior favorably with its policies during the interwar period, especially regarding German reparations.

Bela Balassa suggested that the dollar may be strong because of positive structural changes in the United States—real wage declines, the resolution of the air controllers' strike, deregulation, some "moderation" of social policies—rather than "problems" such as the budget deficit. He also noted that the current account was not as bad as recorded because of the statistical discrepancy. Juergen B. Donges argued that the consolidated budget deficit, including those of state and local governments, was not so bad—although Feldstein replied that the budgets of the local authorities had not changed from the late 1970s.

Jeffrey D. Sachs agreed with Feldstein that the US situation was unsustainable, and that the dollar would eventually have to depreciate, but noted that the United States would later "give back" some of the gains on inflation (once the dollar falls) at much lower inflation rates than in 1981. Therefore, it might have paid for the United States to "export" inflation (via a strong currency) in the early 1980s, and reimport some of that inflation later on, when the inflation is less costly to the economy. Masaru Yoshitomi argued that the US recovery seemed to be investment-oriented, due perhaps to the tax changes of 1981. He therefore wondered whether there was really much "crowding out" and whether the situation might not be largely sustainable. (In response, Feldstein noted that the tax cuts primarily affected personal income, not investment, especially after the alterations of 1982.)

Several speakers expressed the view that the US situation was adverse for the rest of the world. Mihaly Simai and Rehman Sobhan deplored the resultant redistribution of world income to the United States, and Armin Gutowski noted the expansion of American consumption at foreigners' expense. Thierry de Montbrial doubted that the situation was politically sustainable.

Sachs noted the negative impact of high interest rates and negative terms of trade effects, especially for the LDCs. John Williamson, contrary to Feldstein, argued that the strong dollar hurts Latin American exports and that only the US recovery had enabled them to expand their sales. Tony Killick advanced the view that US policies deepened the requirement for retrenchment in the developing world. Bergsten, with Feldstein, emphasized that the strong dollar fostered protectionism in the United States, which could subsequently limit the exports of other countries.

Concluding this session, Feldstein offered his outlook for the future. The likeliest outcome was action in 1985 that would gradually and predictably bring the budget deficit "very much closer to zero by 1990," producing immediate declines in interest rates and the dollar. A "soft landing," with increases in exports and investment that sustained aggregate demand, was a "possible but not guaranteed" result.

By contrast, a sudden, very large cut in the budget deficit would be "disastrous" and bring on an immediate recession, he said. The key requirement to get the needed decline in interest rates and the dollar was predictability, with assured cuts over time. Total inaction would be "very dangerous," since the world will not finance the United States indefinitely and the inevitable dollar decline would produce a sharp runup in interest rates.

3 European Development and the World Economy

Edmond Malinvaud

Global economic development depends on correction of current imbalances. Western Europe has its share of responsibility both for this problem and its solution. First and foremost, Europe should restore equilibrium in its own economy. It should also promote new rules and practices for international economic and financial relations among governments and, above all, a new sense of obligation of each government toward the rest of the world.

My discussion of the European situation is based on these premises. They are not original. The analysis in this paper mostly follows traditional lines and has substantial support in Europe, but I am expressing personal views and do not represent anyone else on this occasion.

Before discussing domestic European policies and harmonization at the world level, I must describe in broad terms the European situation.

THE END OF EASY GROWTH

Hardly anyone would have dared to predict Europe's fast and prolonged economic growth of the 1950s and 1960s. This expansion, at first a surprise, became part of the expected background for all behavior and decisions once people became accustomed to it.

After the initial phase of reconstruction, economic activity could be assigned new objectives without apparently removing any of the older ones. Two ideas concerning the norms for collective action were taken as granted:

15

- anyone working should be guaranteed against a decrease of purchasing power of his disposable income
- social progress was to be achieved.

These goals were to be reached in a number of ways. Investments were to be made in schools, housing, public transport, and other infrastructure. Inequalities in disposable incomes were to be reduced, particularly for low-wage earners, large families, and old people. Improvements were to be made in protection against illness, accidents, and unemployment; in job security, and in worker participation in the collective decision process.

For many years, these two principles held. Real disposable incomes increased. Social progress did not always and everywhere occur on all fronts, but was on the whole quite substantial. Public budgets increased rapidly, as a consequence, but they were financed by rapid increases in revenue generated mainly by economic growth. In most European countries, public debt was small in the early 1970s. People took steady increases in output and productivity for granted and thought the process could go on indefinitely.

Western Europe was unprepared for the sharp break in economic growth that took place 10 years ago.

For the 10 countries of the European Community (EC), real gross domestic product had increased about 4.7 percent a year since the 1950s but only 2.4 percent between the two oil shocks of 1973 and 1979.[1] Expectations were not quickly revised after the shocks. Economists long underestimated the importance of the change, and the public was still slower to realize what was happening and the implications.

Economic policies, of course, varied from one country to another and from one government to the next within each country. Taking a very broad, retrospective view, however, these policies attempted to maintain the dominant principles of the growth period. The same social objectives were reasserted and new progress was often made. As unemployment increased, it was also better compensated through unemployment insurance systems. The result was an increase in the public deficit and government debt. In most countries the notion that real incomes should not decrease was also maintained, and the indexation of wages on consumer prices was often reinforced. This strengthened inflationary forces and resulted in a sharp decrease of profit rates in industry.

Such a policy response would have been wise had the recession of the 1970s been only temporary. But as this hypothesis looked progressively less and less realistic, governments realized that they had to completely revise the ideas on which their economic policies were based.

Before turning to the present situation, we must look at business response to the changes in the economic environment. The period of fast growth had

---

[1] *European Economy*, no. 9 (July 1981), Commission of the European Communities.

been characterized by expanding markets, quickly increasing labor costs relative to capital, and good profitability. These three factors explained high rates of investment.

The first signs that such trends could not last forever came when profitability declined in the early 1970s in some countries where inflation was not accelerating. Although good measures of profitability are elusive, the price configuration of the 1960s seems to have left a substantial margin between the net profit rate in productive operations and the real interest rate. (I have evaluated this margin for French private nonfinancial corporations at 3.5 percent a year on average.)[2] But the push of labor costs in the late 1960s and early 1970s had to either be accommodated by inflation and devaluation or erode profit margins. The precise time when profitability significantly fell varied a good deal from one country to another, but it was low everywhere in 1982, even after rough correction for what may have been due to the unfavorable cyclical component.

In the 1960s European firms were faced with quickly expanding markets, resulting from the growth of world demand, the opening of new markets in neighboring European countries, and the domestic expansion. After the first oil shock, businessmen were not only reluctant to revise downward their expectations but were also fast to seize opportunities in the new markets appearing in the Middle East, in oil-producing countries more generally, and in other parts of the world where, for one reason or another, buyers could get large credits, in Latin America and Eastern Europe in particular. To some extent until 1980 this counteracted the contraction of domestic demand, at least in investment goods industries. But, of course, expectations had to be progressively revised, particularly after the second oil shock and the stabilization programs that large indebted countries had to adopt. European business expectations about future growth now seem even more pessimistic than a reasonable assessment of future prospects would suggest.

The increase of labor costs through the 1960s and 1970s was the consequence of the two commonly accepted principles mentioned at the beginning of this section. One may even add that the achievement of social objectives not only raised wages and payroll taxes or employer social security contributions, but also introduced constraints and rigidities in labor management that were tantamount to an extra increase in costs. Up to the mid-1970s the trend was also toward a reduction of capital costs; real interest rates were low most of the time, and the taxation of productive capital was reduced in various ways. Hence, the cost of labor relative to capital was quickly increasing. The trend was reversed about five years ago at different moments in different countries. Capital costs increased sharply as real interest rates rose and the

---

[2] Edmond Malinvaud, *Essais sur la théorie du chômage* (Paris: Calmann-Lévy, 1983).

rate of labor cost increase slowed down. One may, however, wonder whether the business community is fully aware of this change.

European industrial investment was high for many years by historical standards, even compared to industrial investment elsewhere, except in the fast-growing Far East (and Eastern Europe where it is notoriously inefficient). From 1974 it decreased almost continuously up to 1983, except for a rather short upturn in 1979 and 1980.

WESTERN EUROPE TODAY

Any understanding of Europe's current policy options and position in international debates requires an awareness of the economies' three major problems: unemployment is likely to be high for a number of years and its containment must be given some priority; European competitiveness is uncertain but remains a precondition for any expansion; a sustainable long-term equilibrium must again be found for public budgets, relative prices, and income distribution.

With an average unemployment rate exceeding 10 percent in the EC countries, the present labor surplus is clear and in contrast with the labor shortage prevailing 20 years ago. This labor surplus is not likely to be quickly absorbed. The supply of labor will keep increasing steadily, and the demand for labor will hardly be able to grow at the same speed, much less grow faster as it ought to do in the present situation.

Increases in the working age population and in the number of working women have expanded the labor supply in the past. The demographic structure is such that annual increments in the working age population will remain important for a decade but will decrease slowly from now on. Women's behavior is largely determined by the appearance on the labor market of young generations that have no reason to act differently from their immediate predecessors and will replace older generations whose participation in the labor force was much more limited. Thus, current labor supply projections will likely materialize: an average annual growth of 0.7 percent in the EC countries (Greece excluded) between now and 1990 after 0.9 percent on average since 1975.[3]

The demand for labor will depend on trends of output and labor productivity. Increases in the number of government employees can no longer be expanded to sustain employment as they did somewhat after the first oil shock. Uncertainties are larger about this side of the labor market. During the past decade European output was constrained mainly by the requirement for balance of payments equilibrium, basically for European competitiveness, about which

---

[3] *European Economy*, no. 9 (July 1981), p. 70.

more will be said below. In all likelihood, the same constraint will apply for many years.

Labor productivity has been increasing in Europe during the past decade more slowly than it did 20 years ago. This slowdown is easily explained. In France, for instance, the slackening of industrial productivity can be traced to the aging of equipment and the reduction in its time in use each year, as well as to the lag between employment and output.[4] Moreover, over the past 10 years employment expanded only in services, where productivity gains are low. The reasons for a progressive slowdown have not yet disappeared, so that, extrapolating recent trends, a further small decline can be expected in the rate of increase of labor productivity. If no significant change occurs in business conditions, production per man-hour in the EC (Greece excluded) can still be expected to increase at least 2 percent a year. Output would have to increase around 3 percent a year just to hold unemployment at its present level.

The question must be raised of whether the employment policy of firms will change and whether working hours in coming years will be reduced. Real labor costs are unlikely to increase as much as they did during the past decade; they may even decrease slightly. Flexibility must be restored in labor management, which the social partners seem to accept. We shall return to these issues when discussing internal European policy options.

But is unemployment really a problem after all? West European societies turn out to be much more tolerant of it than anyone would have expected. This is in part because the unemployed receive income compensation and in part because families today often have more than one income earner. This tolerance may also be a reaction to what is now felt to have been public overemphasis in the past.

Despite this tolerance, dismissing the concern about unemployment would be both ethically objectionable and positively unwise. The consequences of prolonged mass unemployment are too wide-ranging to be permanently forgotten by the public. Sooner or later people in Western Europe will want a solution to this problem and, if no improvement is in sight, who knows how the vote will swing?

The solution of the European unemployment problem mainly depends on European competitiveness. Indeed, the option of protectionism would be neither wise nor feasible for Europe. It would be unwise because European demand for minerals and energy is substantial and quite inelastic, whereas demand for European manufactured exports is highly price elastic. Europe thus has much more to lose than to gain in a protectionist struggle among continents. Moreover, the low degree of coordination between the policies of the various European

---

[4] G. Cette and P. Joly, "La productivité industrielle en crise: une interprétation," *Economie et Statistique* (May 1984).

governments makes European protectionism unfeasible except through the independent choice of a protectionist policy by most governments; but then protectionism would also concern intra-European trade and result in an important decline of productivity and standards of living, a decline that European people do not want.

The prevailing view about European competitiveness is definitely pessimistic.[5] Three major handicaps allegedly affecting Europe at this time cause concern. First, the specialization of industry is supposedly leading to a progressive narrowing of the European market share. European industry would be squeezed between the gradual loss of competitiveness and market shares in traditional manufactures to new industrial countries on one hand, and on the other by its inability to compete with North America and Japan in the expanding market for high technology goods. Investment in research and development of new industries is said to have been much too small in Europe. Europe has missed out on "the third industrial revolution," pessimists say.

Second, the European economy has allegedly lost the flexibility it had 30 years ago. Social policies and the pressures from interest groups have resulted in many rigidities hampering management of labor and the allocation of capital. European firms can no longer seize opportunities as they appear, except on a rather limited scale or at a slow pace.

Third, Europeans allegedly no longer give any priority to work. They are more concerned with other dimensions of life. Neither a substantial growth in labor productivity at the macroeconomic level nor a willingness to make exceptional efforts in times when they would be particularly rewarding at the microeconomic level can be expected.

Such a pessimistic view is probably not shared by everybody. In particular, those economists who think that equilibrium always holds cannot even understand the concept of competitiveness. Those who think that disequilibrium can only come from government intervention have an easy solution: remove these interventions. But few people indeed believe the problem is that simple.

Perhaps, however, the pessimistic view is overreacting to some real recent European difficulties or handicaps. The picture it draws may be too black. It reminds me of the picture that was drawn of the French handicaps in the early 1950s, on the eve of the great French expansion. An outside observer might note that the rate of increase of labor productivity is still high in Europe, compared, for instance, to the United States. Unperceived competitive advantages, if undervaluation of European currencies persists, might show up in

---

[5] See, for instance, *Economie mondiale 1980-1990: la fracture?* (Paris: CEPII, May 1984). See also the comments concerning Europe in Assar Lindbeck, "The Recent Slowdown of Productivity Growth," and Herbert Giersch and F. Wolter, "Toward an Explanation of the Productivity Slowdown: An Acceleration-Deceleration Hypothesis," both in *Economic Journal* (March 1983).

coming years. But such an optimistic turn is still less likely than the pessimistic perspective most commonly accepted.

European economic disequilibria became particularly apparent after the second oil shock, which was compounded by the strong appreciation of the dollar and of dollar-priced basic commodities. But the present orientation of economic policies seems to be such as to lead to a reabsorption of almost all these disequilibria, the exception being, of course, unemployment. This appears to apply to inflation, balances of payments, public budgets, and industrial profitability.

In their fight against inflation, various European governments responded differently. Some were particularly tolerant of inflation during the 1970s. In some countries, not only was wage indexation on the consumer price index made more systematic, but substantial wage increases above the resulting level were also granted, which could only result in an acceleration of the inflationary process. This tolerance has now been replaced by a definite desire for low rates of wage and price increase. Thus, inflation is receding and the risk of its shooting up again has been definitely lowered. For the EC countries as a whole (excluding Greece), the annual rate of increase in consumer prices was 3.3 percent in 1965–67, 6 percent in 1970–72, 13 percent in 1974, 7.2 percent in 1978, 11.1 percent in 1980, and about 5.1 percent in 1984. Analysts of the medium-term future are rather cautious in their forecasts and anticipate only a slow further decrease. They may well be underestimating the structural change that occurred in the most inflation-prone West European countries.

For the casual observer, the ex post aggregate West European balance of payments is not a subject for concern. This balance indeed appeared more often in surplus than deficit. For the nine EC countries, the surplus on current operations amounted to 0.8 percent of GDP in 1971–72; the deficits following from the two oil shocks (− 0.8 in 1974 and − 1.3 in 1980 as a percentage of GDP) were quickly reabsorbed (0.9 percent in 1978 and 0.2 percent in 1984). Those are, of course, ex post and aggregated figures. Each European country taken by itself considers its economic policy to be subject to serious balance of payment constraints; and certain countries at times ran large balance of payment deficits (Italy and the United Kingdom in 1974, West Germany in 1980, France in 1982, to mention only the large countries). The figures show, however, that the recent trend has been toward better control of deficits. In 1983 deficits and surpluses were moderate in all Common Market countries. The forecasts for 1984 and 1985 confirm the absence in Europe of any major deficit country.

Europe's public finance dilemma is not so much over high budget deficits and heavy government debts but rather over ever-increasing social transfers and public resistance to ever-increasing taxation. But a solution to this problem is underway, though still in its initial stages. Net borrowings by government have begun to decrease as a share of GDP, and the increase of public expenditures is being curbed.

As a share of GDP, net government borrowing in the nine EC countries averaged 4 percent between 1975 and 1983, higher than the corresponding US figure. This large deficit was first due to deliberate countercyclical fiscal policy in 1975; but its more recent high level (4.6 percent of GDP in 1982 and 1983) is well explained by increased interest payments and social transfers related to unemployment, whereas since 1979 the ex ante stance of fiscal policies has become more restrictive in most countries.[6] The ratio of the government borrowing to GDP decreased to 4.3 percent in 1984 and is expected to decrease further to 3.7 percent in 1985.

The main challenge to policymakers is to succeed in reducing this deficit still further while stopping, and even reversing, the rising trend of taxation (including social security contributions). Indeed, from 1975 to 1982, current resources of government in relation to GDP increased by 5 percentage points, owing to an equal increase in government and social security transfers, while public consumption as a share of GDP increased by 1 point, but government fixed capital formation decreased by 1 point.[7]

The social consensus seems to be that this simultaneous increase in taxation and transfers went too far and must now be somewhat reversed. How this will be done is far from clear, since consensus disappears on specific measures to curb the growth of health services, old age pensions, or unemployment benefits. In fact, stringent measures have already been taken, a good many of them bearing not on social transfers but on government subsidies to business, on public consumption, and on public investment. However, these measures cannot yet be considered as fully meeting the challenge. If I maintain that European public finance disequilibria will be reduced in the coming years, it is because I perceive a determined will to achieve this objective, not because I see precisely how it will be done.

The deterioration of industrial profitability culminated in 1981 when profit rates were low and real interest rates high. The well-known evolution of real interest rates will not be stressed any more here, except to mention that current rates are now kept definitely lower in Western Europe than in North America. The noteworthy point is that profit rates have recovered in Europe.

Good measures of this recent phenomenon are not yet available; its examination requires statistics that are obtained only with a substantial lag. But the phenomenon is strong enough to appear clearly on all the available proxy indicators. For instance, between 1981 and 1983 the share of labor cost

---

[6] See R. W. R. Price and J.-C. Chouraqui, "Public Sector Deficits: Problems and Implications," OECD, *Occasional Studies* (June 1983).

[7] *OECD Economic Outlook*, no. 35 (July 1984).

in industrial value added is estimated to have decreased from 78 percent to 72.4 percent in West Germany and from 82.3 percent to 80.5 percent in France, where, however, the restoration started later and will show much more strongly on the 1984 results.[8] This recent trend follows from a definite change in the deterioration of wages, a change that corrects the European wage gap, which was much talked about until recently.

The prospect of thus seeing almost all Europe's economic disequilibria resolved has, of course, to do with the currently favorable phase of the North American business cycle which is mildly spreading to Europe. Things would be made more difficult if in 1985 the leading economy went into recession and debtor countries had to apply more severe policies than the existing ones. From a broad perspective, however, one phase of Europe's economic evolution is ending. A new phase is opening, whose outcome will depend both on European economic policies and on the worldwide context.

THE EUROPEAN RESPONSE

Turning to this coming phase, attention must be shifted to the formulation of normative prescriptions that are feasible considering Europe's institutional features. To be sure, such prescriptions will depend on who formulates them, how the working of the economic system is seen, how the choice is made in the trade-off between conflicting aims. I therefore remind you that I speak just for myself.

To solve the unemployment problem while strengthening the equilibria soon to be restored, the appropriate policy package can only be mixed, both because feasible or acceptable margins of action are often narrow and because strong actions would be disequilibrating in one way or another. As I see it, this is the appropriate policy mix:

- find the proper medium-term equilibrium path for relative prices, public finance, and social security schemes
- reintroduce flexibility in adjustments to changing circumstances, particularly on the labor market
- use European cooperation to improve competitiveness and reflate moderately
- take specific measures for the period of mass unemployment.

I have claimed that, except for unemployment, major European disequilibria are being reduced. Assuming this bold thesis has been accepted (I easily imagine that it is hard to swallow for some of my European colleagues who are

---

[8] *Economie mondiale 1980-1990: la fracture?* (Paris: CEPII, May 1984). See also *OECD Economic Outlook*, no. 35 (July 1984).

struggling to make the process effective), where should the corrections go? Profit margins should not become excessive after their excessive squeeze; social protection should not be slashed right after being made so extensive that it has become unsustainable.

The question may still appear to be premature because in some respects, for instance, in public finance, the corrections still have a good way to go in the obvious direction. However, answering the question correctly is a difficult challenge for economists, who have to ascertain the range of feasible equilibrium paths; politicians and voters, who have to make the proper choice among these paths; and administrators, who have to help to effectuate the one chosen. Considering such difficulties, time is short.

The existence of a problem is widely recognized concerning the social security schemes to be applied during the next one or two decades. Its major components are known: pattern of old age pensions, level of family allowances, social cost of medicare and health services, schemes of unemployment insurance. The existing systems often have to be revised both to control increases in their costs and to avoid, or at least curtail, some of their disincentive effects. These revisions will not be easy either to decide or to implement. To a remote observer they may, however, look quite manageable.

It is less widely recognized that some reconsideration of the fiscal systems will also have to occur sooner or later. While the generalization of the progressive income tax in the interwar period and the value-added tax in the postwar period were definite achievements, the present state of corporate and private capital taxation is quite messy. As a result of subsidizations and impositions of various kinds, introduced helter skelter without due consideration of their interference with previously existing ones, the taxation package today makes little sense and cannot be considered conducive to balanced, equitable, and efficient growth.

But the main question is to which target should the functional income distribution and the costs of labor and capital aim? Indeed, policymakers cannot consider it as a purely academic question, since shifts in income distribution and input costs are not determined only by the changing features of market equilibrium but also by economic policies.

Both the supply side and the demand side need attention. On the supply side two main indicators should be watched: the relative cost of labor with respect to capital and the pure profit margin in productive operations, or perhaps better, the ratio between the net profit rate earned in these operations and the real interest rate. On the demand side, the question should be addressed of whether induced consumption and investment demand meets employment and balance of payments requirements.

Within this large agenda for prospective studies I consider one point particularly crucial: should the target for the pure profit rate in the second half of the 1980s be the same as during the 1960s in the European countries that did well? The situation has changed and may call for fresh analysis. Investment needs are different and probably smaller, even though the lags of the past decade should be made up; indeed, the growth of output will be quite significantly slower. But investment may be more risky and therefore require the extra incentive of high pure profit margins; it may appear more risky both because of the larger uncertainties of the world economy and because it should be concentrated in new industries, where Europe is starting off with a handicap. Confronted with these two conflicting considerations, intuition may well suggest that the profitability level of the 1960s is an appropriate target after all.

Concern about restoring incentives extends beyond business profitability into concern about reintroducing flexibility, so that the economy can adapt much more quickly to changing circumstances than it now does.

Such renewed profitability and flexibility would be favorable for two reasons. It would improve competitiveness, which is crucial for stimulating the growth of output. It would also lead to higher employment for any given output level, since higher profitability and flexibility induce firms to be less cautious in their recruitment policy.

To a large extent, promoting incentives and flexibility is reversing the trend of the past 30 years. This means both changing the previously prevailing public opinion on these matters and reducing the power of the pressure groups that often determined the changes that reduced incentives and introduced rigidities. Neither is easy.

Optimists say that pressure groups will have to modify their demands or be left behind after public opinion changes, as it must, in the reality of the prohibitive economic and social costs of rigidity and protection. This view is optimistic but not unrealistic, considering the recent evolution of ideas and common experience in Europe. Significantly, the EC Economic Policy Committee has written a position paper on the why and how of improving flexibility of the labor market.

To implement this policy orientation, and to do it in a way that minimizes its unfavorable effects with respect to certain social objectives, many aspects of institutions, law, regulations, and their application within each European country have to be reconsidered. Remuneration patterns naturally come to mind, including legislation on minimum wages, career protection, lay off or dismissal of workers, unemployment insurance, housing, retraining facilities, and the like. But other issues also need to be rethought concerning capital markets, antitrust laws, and agricultural policies, to name just a few.

It would be pointless to go into detail here about some of the advisable reforms. Only the policy orientation and the commitment to implement it matter. We should simply be aware of the many facets that have to be dealt with and the difficulty of choosing among unpleasant trade-offs. Implementation will take time; the impact on competitiveness and employment will take still more time. This is a long-term affair.

Cooperation and coordination of economic policies within Europe is needed more now than ever before. Progress in high technology industries as well as orderly and moderate reflation depend on it.

For the long-term future of the European economy, Europe must be at the cutting edge of technological development and make up for any past lags. It is hardly debatable that such lags resulted, partly at least, from divisions between European countries. Wars have benefited only the weapons-producing industries. Today economies of scale in research, development, and application of some new technologies are substantial and give a definite advantage to integrated large economies.

Europe's technological lag should not be overemphasized, since it is performing well in a number of cases, and European cooperation already exists. But more should be done to regain competitiveness in some products with quickly expanding markets.

Assuming a fairly good European competitive position, there will be room for stimulating demand after the present phase of disinflation ends. Considering the trend toward still higher unemployment, we must take advantage of change. In the process, two principles must be respected: demand management must be moderate, and it must be coordinated between countries.

Experience shows that, even when unemployment is high, strong demand push stimulates not only output but also inflation. This may be particularly true for Western Europe now, because poor profitability has led, for a number of years now, to scrapping many old productive capacities while building few new ones. A strong surge of demand would run into many equipment bottlenecks, and inflation would accelerate. This can be avoided if stimulation is moderate but steady.

On the other hand, maintaining and consolidating a large, integrated West European market with stable relative exchange rates is basic for good business performance and limited risks. These conditions would attract the necessary investment to both serve foreign markets and permit further expansion. This investment climate would not last long if the economic policies of the various countries were too divergent. Good coordination of these policies must be sought.

Moreover, demand stimulation clearly will not occur unless most European governments simultaneously decide on it. One or two countries alone cannot effectively do it because of the deficit that would soon disturb the balance of foreign trade. Concerted action is required.

Even under the best of circumstances, European unemployment will remain high until the beginning of the 1990s. Economic policy has to find ways of accommodating this situation. This means that unconventional measures to curb unemployment may have to be considered, and perhaps adopted. Indeed, some such measures have been taken during the past 10 years such as early retirement, reduced working time, and employment subsidies.

A number of my fellow economists are suspicious of such measures, to say the least. Government intervention of this type looks to them like interference with the free play of the economic system, undermining its efficiency. These economists systematically reject the kind of measures I am now considering.

I must say it gives me no pleasure to take so different a stand. While I am less convinced than others of the virtues of a free economy (whatever that means), I agree that government intervention is potentially inefficient, and I should prefer a situation where it did not have to be seriously discussed. But mass unemployment is a major inefficiency. Measures to reduce it may be advisable even if they induce other inefficiencies. In the present case, as in many others, one can only aim at second best.

Here, the main objective should be to fashion accommodating decisions in a way that best reduces unemployment with least damage to long-term economic efficiency. The real danger then is either that the consequences of the measures to be adopted are misevaluated, or that distortions occur within the political process, and that the final decisions turn out to be very different from the second-best ones.

THE INTERNATIONAL ORDER

For more than a decade, the working of the international economy has not been satisfactory. Indeed, the question of what to do about it has been posed many times, more or less violently. Because answers are so elusive, it needs particularly serious study.

In this debate Western Europe has an important voice, not only because of its self-interest in the working of the international economy but also because of its long standing involvement with the subject. I must try here to express what I may perceive to be a majority European view. No doubt, my interpretation would be disputed by at least some other Europeans.

Though painful for Europe in the short run, the present imbalances might turn out to be favorable in the long run, if maintained. An overvalued dollar raises the cost of European imports, and demand for European exports is depressed by the strict adjustment policies that debtor countries have to adopt to service their debts at high interest rates. On the other hand, an overvalued dollar enhances Europe's market position, and lower real interest rates in Europe than in the United States stimulate productive investment in Europe. Perhaps a slow world economy also increases European industry's chances of catching up in the technological race where its weakness is now apparent.

But of course the present imbalances will not be maintained. The main feature of the international economic system is its instability, not that it overvalues the dollar (although it does) nor that it necessarily leads to high American interest rates. The effective exchange rate of the dollar will not remain at its present level. The behavior of money and capital markets, reacting in particular to government economic policies, but not to those only, will certainly lead to new surprises affecting interest rates. The price of oil and other basic materials may be expected to fluctuate violently again.

This instability is disruptive in itself. Economic agents, aware of this instability, now have to be cautious; this in turn induces, at the aggregate level, low growth and high unemployment. This current contraction is especially painful because of its late arrival, after excessive optimism in the late 1960s and early 1970s, after excessive financial risk-taking in the late 1970s. Past mistakes must now be paid for. A safe business climate would help head off too long a period of economic stagnation.

Risks abound. Thus far, pressures for protectionism have been more or less contained;[9] at least their effect has been limited, and international trade is still strong. But protectionist options have not yet been written off by businessmen suffering from acute foreign competition, by governments confronted with industrial redevelopment problems, or by citizens sensitive to unemployment in their countries. Long-term damage can easily be imagined from further, extensive, and swift protectionist action, mainly of the nontariff sort. World economic instability clearly enhances the attractiveness of protectionism; anything that reduces this instability will also lower the probability of increased protectionism.

Europe's voice in the debate for international economic order then mainly focuses on the advisability and feasibility of stabilizing reform. But it also speaks on two other issues: the conditions to be met to give the poorer half of the human race a chance and the need for a long-term perspective on some important aspects of future economic activity.

Economists cannot help thinking about the economic problems that the large populations in the poorest countries of the world will face. There is no point berating Europe for its past role in shaping these countries' present situation. Human solidarity on the planet should give the main motivation for action.

Development problems may not be mainly economic. Their economic components cannot be easily solved, all the more so as some misconceptions about the causes of the difficulties still receive widespread attention. Moreover, the populations and governments of the countries involved have to decide for

---

[9] See, for instance, Shirley Williams, "Unemployment and Economic Strains in the Western Alliance," in *Unemployment and Growth in the Western Economies*, edited by A. J. Pierre (New York: Council on Foreign Relations, 1984).

themselves. But, in an interdependent world, their scope of action and the results of their decisions also depend on our behavior.

Except for direct assistance in extreme cases and rescue operations to starving populations, which should not be forgotten, our responsibility can be summarized by the three following rules:

- provide a secure international environment
- transmit the appropriate know-how
- accept the consequences of Third World development.

The first rule stresses the objective of stabilizing the world economy and the advisability of realistic long-term perspectives. The second one concerns issues outside the domain to be considered in this paper. The third one implies that certain responses to European difficulties should be avoided. While a high level of activity in the industrial countries is favorable to the Third World and may require the easing of some industrial adjustment by specific, temporary relief, the long-term evolution necessary for the development of poor countries should be accepted. This is another reason to oppose protectionism.

Reducing world economic instability, not to mention restoring stability, is, of course, difficult. The presence of imbalances is not an accident. It is rather a natural consequence of large international flows of goods and capital, the institutional framework in which they take place, and finally the experience acquired by businessmen and other people over the past 20 years. The institutional framework in particular has many features, many of them not intended, most of them favorable since they permitted a fast expansion of international trade.

Difficult or not, reducing instability is important. It is really intolerable to hear it said, time and again, that the problem does not exist, as if the present situation were satisfactory, as if there were nothing to do about it. The first step in an international program against economic instability, then, is explicit recognition of the problem and expression of the will to attack it. This has been called "the Bretton Woods spirit," which has indeed been lacking during the past 10 years.

It would be presumptuous here, and useless at this stage, to present a well-defined program for the institutional changes that ought to be accepted and implemented. Clearly, this program will restrict the freedom of action of national monetary authorities, since the use of monetary policy for the fulfillment of national objectives sometimes conflicts with the requirements of international stability. Such constraints on monetary policies should find their place within a preagreed pattern, under a control that the International Monetary Fund (IMF) is well suited to assume.

The constraints will particularly concern US monetary policy, for the simple reason that the dollar is in some respects close to being the money of the world. The dollar is no longer simply the American people's money. In 1971 some of us thought the dollar would lose part of its international role and leave room to some other national currencies. We were wrong; the international use of American money has kept on increasing.

Is it fair to impose stronger monetary policy restrictions on the American people than are imposed on others? This question is not relevant. When a team is exposed to danger and only one member of the team is able to ward off this danger, no one asks whether it is fair to expose him alone. Moreover, if the American seigniorage imposes special duties, it also has some advantages for the American people.

Deciding on institutional reforms to reduce international monetary instability will take time. Before any agreement, governments and people of leading countries ought to become accustomed to paying more attention to the international consequences of their policies. This may well conflict in the short run with selfish concern for their own interest; but in the long run, considering how interdependent nations have become, this may nevertheless be shrewd strategy, even from the limited viewpoint of a single country.

Attention to the international consequences of individual actions would be fostered by tightening coordination of economic policies. This may also both give each government some guarantee about the international environment and permit some compensation for particular sacrifices made by one country or another.

Prescience would, of course, help considerably to prevent some imbalances in the world economy from emerging, particularly the financial ones. Unfortunately, it is not accessible. But, contrary to what is sometimes said, "the market" does not fully transmit all the information available about the future. Indeed, other means already exist for the emergence and transmission of economic information. Improving them would play a significant role.

This is particularly true about long-term trends, which cannot be sensibly detected from prices formed in what are essentially shortsighted markets. Relevant information concerns quantitative data about demand and supplies in commodity and labor markets, but also price data about exchange rates, real interest rates, prices of oil and other basic commodities. Improved information on these trends would lead economic agents to wiser long-term decisions.

Improving techniques for gathering, analyzing, and disseminating long-term forecasting information will be neither easy nor fast, but the matter is too important to be neglected. The will to do something about it should be constant. One possible approach might embody this concern within the preparation of a program for international monetary reform, as indeed was in the mind of some of the Bretton Woods negotiators.

Chapter 3   Discussion

Herbert Giersch suggested that Europe benefited in the 1950s and 1960s from exceptionally favorable conditions, such as trade liberalization and open markets during the reconstruction period after World War II, cheaply imported technology from the United States, an export-led growth promoted by US economic policy, and lagging wages due to labor organizations that could not keep pace with the expansion of markets and the growth of labor productivity. The result was an extraordinary catching-up process within just two decades.

Such rapid expansion, however, could not be sustained forever. When the accelerated growth process ran into supply bottlenecks, the correction of distorted price ratios, as between wages and profits, took the form of an overshooting. Europe, and especially West Germany, experienced a sharp cost push due to a strong movement toward higher real wages (a "revolt of labor") at the end of the 1960s with a simultaneous march into the welfare state, and higher relative prices for energy and other nonrenewable resources (a "land revolt") which arose with the first oil crisis in the early 1970s. This cost push coincided with the upward revaluation of the European currencies against the dollar after the collapse of the Bretton Woods system.

One policy response was an accommodating monetary policy intended to cushion the impact of the various shocks on profits which, however, reduced the real rate of interest through unanticipated inflation, resulting in a great waste of capital in housing, excessively capital-intensive investment, and depressed saving. This at last pushed up real rates of interest and thus led to a "counterrevolution of capital." Moreover, the widespread reliance on government's help through protectionism and subsidies led to a decline in the general motivation level and the readiness to adjust. Europe since then has suffered from economic sclerosis which ought to be called "Eurosclerosis."

As a result, Europe finds itself in a less healthy economic environment than that of the United States or Japan. Europe's growth potential for the next few years is no more than 2 percent annually—compared with around 4 percent for the United States.

Professor Giersch offered a series of proposals to remedy the situation. First, labor markets needed to become much more flexible. Relative wages were the key; they were often too high at the entry level, but too low for high skills. Newly established firms should be excepted from minimum wage hikes resulting from collective bargaining. Correspondingly, Giersch opposed such steps as reductions in the work week, earlier retirement, or a larger role for labor unions.

In addition, Europe should imitate the United States by actively pursuing deregulation, he suggested, as many industries are still regulated at the national level. Tax rates should be eased for new firms to promote the development of venture capital, and high marginal rates should be cut to improve incentives. All these steps could be taken at the national level; there was no need to stress common EC action. Giersch argued that Europe was "five years behind the United States" in achieving economic revitalization. (Masaru Yoshitomi subsequently asked, if this was the case, was the dollar really "overvalued"?)

Concerning macroeconomic policy, Professor Giersch concurred in measures to expand demand, but only if they were accompanied by the more structural steps cited. He advocated trade liberalization to help promote the needed structural changes. In that same vein, Jeffrey D. Sachs later asked why there were not more policy trade-offs in Europe between structural reform and stimulative demand policies. By contrast, Yoshitomi wondered whether macro stimulus was needed at all if the structural reforms were undertaken.

Finally, Giersch concluded that the overvaluation of the dollar was a net benefit to Europe, because the excessively high relative price of European labor was thus corrected via the exchange rate, at least vis-à-vis US competitors. If lasting, a dollar overvaluation would also stimulate US direct investment in Europe.

In the general discussion, Francis Cripps expressed doubt over Malinvaud's thesis that Europe needed to emphasize improving its international competitive position. He pointed out that Europe itself offered quite a large market, that there was less direct competition than usually thought between Europe and the rest of the world, and that Europe should not mind if North America and Asia got together more extensively. He argued against a "US-centered" analysis of the world economy, suggesting that Europe was underestimating its own potential—including its effect on the United States and other countries.

Sachs addressed the United Kingdom specifically, suggesting that no basic economic gains had been made to date under the Thatcher government. Some uncompetitive firms had been eliminated, but no new capacity had been put in place. Full-employment productivity had not risen and may even have declined.

Balassa was also quite pessimistic about Europe. He saw no persuasive signs that productivity was growing faster in Europe than in the United States. Even Europe's small labor productivity gains were due to increased capital-to-labor ratios. Profits had declined substantially. Labor was costing firms as much as three times its value to them in Sweden and even Germany. Wages per unit of output were still rising.

Stephen Marris expressed doubt about the "Europessimism" enunciated by Giersch. Profits had recovered sharply since 1981, especially in Germany. How could one know that Europe could not grow faster than 2 percent unless one tried? A 2 percent "ceiling" could not be placed. Marris noted that pessimism had been widespread in the United States as recently as 1982, but that policy stimulus had led to rapid growth shortly thereafter. Noting that Europe had grown by about 5 percent in 1978–79, he wondered whether all these rigidities had developed "overnight" and argued that Europe could have grown faster during the previous two years.

Marris did suggest that time might "be running short." The American boom would end someday, leaving Europe (and other countries) to expand on their own. Willem H. Buiter endorsed this view, arguing that Europe's most important current need was to develop a coordinated contingency plan against the next American recession. Marris supported Giersch's structural recommendations but advocated simultaneous action to stimulate demand. Osman Okyar added that apparent rigidities and psychological barriers could reverse quickly, as recently in Turkey (particularly with respect to state ownership). W. Max Corden later noted that fiscal expansion had worked in Australia despite some structural problems similar to those in Europe.

Rimmer de Vries asked whether the gap between Europe and the United States was increasing or decreasing. If the former, the dollar would continue to rise. He doubted that Europe was ready for expansionary measures, and therefore concluded that the United States had better continue providing the major locomotion.

In a final comment, Giersch reemphasized the view that monetary expansion in Europe would be effective only after the needed structural changes had occurred. At that point, monetary policy could achieve the required stimulus without fiscal expansion, although he did support tax cuts for supply-side reasons.

4 Japan's View of Current External Imbalances

Masaru Yoshitomi

Japan's changing position in the international financial system has received less attention than its role in the trading system. The Japanese economy has emerged as a large exporter of capital and savings based on its chronic current account surplus. This changing position of Japan has, however, been obscured by a growing and extraordinarily large external imbalance in its current account with the United States and also by the Keynesian-oriented policy implications of this imbalance for macroeconomic management in Japan.

A FEW KEY QUESTIONS

This paper discusses several key issues. First is the unique character of the sectoral savings investment (SI) imbalance in Japan which warrants the coexistence of high-employment (or cyclically adjusted) government deficits and a high-employment current account surplus. Second is the appropriate direction of Japan's fiscal policy in the context both of Japan's high-employment government deficit and a large and growing current account deficit in the United States. While countercyclical fiscal policies are to be aimed at smoothing out cyclical fluctuations of domestic output without risking medium- and long-run

This paper is derived partly from the author's paper "Japan as a Capital Exporter and the World Economy," prepared for the Group of Thirty (June 1984). The opinions expressed here represent the opinions of the author and have not been officially endorsed by any institution of which he is, or has been, a member.

aftermaths (for example, the acceleration of inflation and the crowding out of productive investment), a relevant question is not the existence of Japan's external surplus but its magnitude, i.e., the cyclical component of its external surplus, and whether Japan's fiscal policies should be oriented more toward rectifying cyclical external imbalances.

Third is the extent to which Japan's real interest rates in the long term can be independent of US real interest rates, once Japan's economy becomes increasingly integrated with the world capital market under floating exchange rates. Japan has become more fully integrated with international capital markets through domestic liberalization of exchange controls and financial regulations. If long-run interest parity prevails with perfect substitutability between home (Japan) and foreign (US) bonds, domestic real interest rates in Japan may not be so independent from US real interest rates. This may impel Japan toward international macroeconomic coordination.

HIGH EMPLOYMENT, GOVERNMENT DEFICIT, AND CURRENT ACCOUNT SURPLUS

In determining whether the Japanese economy has established itself as a capital exporter on a basis of a chronic current account surplus, the question arises of whether the surplus is caused by low domestic demand in Japan and whether it can be eliminated or reduced by an expansionary fiscal policy. Stated another way, will the current account remain in surplus even when the Japanese economy is at high employment?

This concept of the high-employment current account surplus is analogous to the high-employment government deficit. While the high-employment government deficit is customarily referred to as peculiar to a closed economy, the high-employment current account surplus may be defined as peculiar to an open economy. The domestic business cycle causes not only cyclical budget imbalances but also cyclical current account imbalances. In addition to such business cycles, world economic conditions, petroleum price changes, and exchange rates also affect the size of the current account imbalance. Hence, the high-employment current account surplus should be defined as the surplus generated when not only domestic output but also world trade, foreign output, and the exchange rate return to normal and natural levels. It is almost impossible, however, to assume a normal or natural level for petroleum prices. In the case of petroleum prices, therefore, the current oil price should be taken and the high-employment surplus in effect should be measured after the economy has largely completed its adjustment to changes in petroleum prices.

Bearing these qualifications in mind, let us examine the nature of Japan's current account surpluses in 1977–78 and 1982–83. By 1977–78 and 1982–83, the Japanese economy had more or less completed its adjustment to oil increases, after the first and second oil shocks, respectively.

TABLE 4.1 HIGH-EMPLOYMENT GOVERNMENT DEFICITS AND HIGH-EMPLOYMENT
PRIVATE SAVINGS-INVESTMENT GAPS, 1970–81
(percentage of high-employment nominal GNP)

Fiscal year	High-employment government deficit (1)	High-employment excess private savings (2)	High-employment current account imbalance of Japan (3)	(4) = (2) - (3)	(Reference)	
					High-employment rate of un-employment (5)	High-employment deficit of the central govt. (6)
1970	1.83	0.71	1.46	−0.75	1.49	−0.59
1971	0.65	2.16	2.30	−0.14	1.54	−0.94
1972	0.78	1.41	1.75	−0.35	1.60	−1.01
1973	2.97	−0.65	−1.27	0.62	1.65	0.61
1974	1.49	−1.41	−1.67	0.25	1.71	1.02
1975	−1.36	2.79	−1.36	4.15	1.77	−1.43
1976	−1.35	1.59	−0.37	1.95	1.83	−2.38
1977	−2.41	2.32	0.96	1.36	1.89	−3.33
1978	−2.02	1.44	0.45	0.98	1.96	−3.63
1979	−3.38	0.97	−1.90	2.87	2.03	−4.99
1980	−3.08	1.63	−1.16	2.79	2.10	−4.90
1981	−3.19	2.65	−0.25	2.90	2.17	n.a.

SOURCE: Economic Planning Agency 1983.

Our estimates (EPA 1983) indicate that the high-employment external surplus accounted for about 0.8 percent of high-employment GNP in 1977–78 on average (table 4.1). These estimates are based on an open macro model of the Japanese economy for 1965–81, where world trade and exchange rates are treated as exogenous variables. In 1977–78, the high-employment government deficit was about 2.2 percent of high-employment GNP. It is difficult to estimate the high-employment current account for 1982–83 by using the above Japanese model because the world economic situation and exchange rates were far from normal or natural levels.

Judging from the multiplier simulations made by using the EPA world econometric model (1984) and a study (Hooper and Tyron 1984) using the MCM (multicountry model), however, we can say the following. In 1982–83, the *actual* external surplus of Japan accounted for 1.4 percent of GNP, for which two nonstructural factors must have worked in a conflicting manner. One factor was the overvalued US dollar (with the undervalued yen as its counterpart), which worked for larger surpluses for Japan. If we suppose that the overvalued US dollar was caused by the macro policy mix in the United States, Japan's current account surplus should be larger by about $9.7 billion than in the absence of such a US macro policy, according to our multiplier simulations. The EPA multiplier simulations indicate that bond-financed fiscal expansion in the United States equivalent to 1 percent of GNP generates an extra $2.6 billion for Japan's current account surplus on average in the second and third years after the initial impact (the scale of 1982–83 figures is 1.5

TABLE 4.2 SUMMARY OF JAPAN'S BALANCE OF PAYMENTS, 1961–83
(billion US dollars)

Year	Current account			Capital account	
	Total account	Investment income		Long-term capital	Short-term capital
		Credits	Debits		
1961	− 1.0	—	0.1	—	0.6
1962	− 0.1	0.1	0.2	0.2	0.2
1963	− 0.8	0.1	0.2	0.5	0.3
1964	− 0.5	0.1	0.3	0.1	0.3
1965	0.9	0.2	0.4	− 0.4	− 0.4
1966	1.3	0.2	0.4	− 0.8	− 0.4
1967	− 0.2	0.3	0.5	− 0.8	0.5
1968	1.1	0.3	0.6	− 0.3	—
1969	2.1	0.5	0.8	− 0.2	− 1.5
1970	2.0	0.7	0.9	− 1.6	− 0.7
1971	5.8	1.0	1.0	− 1.1	5.5
1972	6.6	1.6	1.3	− 4.5	0.2
1973	− 0.1	2.7	2.2	− 9.8	2.4
1974	− 4.7	3.6	4.0	− 3.9	9.9
1975	− 0.7	3.6	3.9	− 0.3	0.8
1976	3.7	3.5	3.7	− 1.0	1.0
1977	10.9	3.7	3.6	− 3.2	− 2.2
1978	16.5	5.3	4.4	− 12.4	5.8
1979	− 8.8	9.0	7.0	− 12.6	6.4
1980	− 10.7	11.1	10.3	2.4	16.4
1981	4.8	15.8	16.5	− 9.7	7.6
1982	6.9	18.4	16.6	− 15.0	− 1.0
1983					

— Negligible.
SOURCE: The Bank of Japan, *Balance of Payments Monthly.*
a. Percentage on a national account basis.

times as large as in the EPA multiplier for 1976–77 nominal figures). Assuming that fiscal expansion was about 2.5 percent of GNP, judging from an increase in the US high-employment government deficit between 1981 and 1983 (De Leeuw and Holloway 1983), we get $9.7 billion as the total addition to Japan's current account surplus attributable to fiscal expansion in the United States.

The other factor that may or may not raise Japan's high-employment current account surplus is the international business cycle in 1982–83. According to the Hooper-Tyron study based on the MCM, the GNP gap between actual and trend was larger for the United States, West Germany, and the United Kingdom because of stagnant output for three consecutive years in the 1980–82 recession, whereas the GNP gap in Japan remained relatively small due to the shallowness of the recession during the same period. Therefore, if the GNP gap narrowed and actual GNP returned to trend GNP in major advanced countries (underlying trend growth is 4 percent for Japan and 2.5

Errors and omissions	Changes in external reserves	Proportion of the current imbalance to nominal GNP[a]
—	0.3	
—	0.3	
—	—	
—	0.1	
—	0.1	1.1
—	—	1.3
—	—	−0.0
—	0.9	0.8
0.1	0.6	1.3
0.3	0.9	−1.1
0.5	10.8	−2.6
0.6	3.1	2.3
−2.6	−6.1	0.0
—	1.3	−0.9
−0.6	−0.7	−0.1
0.1	3.8	−0.7
0.7	6.2	1.6
0.3	10.2	1.8
2.3	−12.7	−0.8
−3.1	4.9	−0.9
0.5	3.2	0.6
4.1	−5.1	0.8
		1.9

percent for others), the higher world trade resulting would enhance Japan's high-employment surplus. If the United States, West Germany, and the United Kingdom each expand fiscal expenditures by 3 percent of GNP to fill their own GNP gap, Japan's current account would improve by $13.5 billion, whereas if Japan expanded fiscal expenditure by 1 percent of GNP to narrow its GNP gap, its current account would worsen by $2.4 billion. The net result would be a $9.5 billion increase of Japan's external surplus.

Thus, the impact on Japan's external surplus of these two forces (the US policy mix and the GNP gap in major advanced countries) should largely offset each other. Consequently, the actual GNP ratio of the current account surplus in 1982–83 (about 1.4 percent) must be close to Japan's high-employment current account surplus. A broad conclusion from the above observations is that Japan's high-employment current account surplus will range from 1 percent to 1.5 percent of GNP, which is equivalent to a net surplus of $12 billion to $18 billion compared with a $1.2 trillion GNP in 1982–83.

To better understand Japan's chronic surplus and position as a capital exporter, it is useful to review the evolution of its balance of payments. The Japanese economy has rather quickly experienced three stages in the evolution of its balance of payments since World War II (table 4.2):

- Stage 1. An immature debtor country with current account deficits, 1945–64.
- Stage 2. A mature debtor country with current account surpluses but still with *net payments* of investment income, 1965–71.
- Stage 3. An immature creditor country with current account surpluses and with *net receipts* of investment income, 1972–present.

In other words, in Stage 1, which lasted 20 years, Japan was an international borrower in both flow and stock terms. In Stage 2, which was a relatively short period, it became an international lender but only in flow terms. Finally, in Stage 3, it has become an international creditor in both flow and stock terms.

In Stage 2, under the adjustable peg exchange rate system, Japan's current account surplus accounted for a rather stable share of nominal GNP—around 1.5 percent on average—except for the last phase (1971–72) of the Bretton Woods system, when the yen became unrealistically undervalued.

In Stage 3, Japan's current account has registered both deficits and surpluses under the floating exchange rate regime. This is attributable to the two oil crises. Table 4.2 shows that in 1974–75 under the first oil shock and also in 1979–80 under the second, the current account was in deficit. But the table also shows more importantly that in both periods and since 1981 large surpluses persisted in the current account. The oil-crisis-induced deficits have been more than offset by the surpluses since 1981, but the cumulative current account surplus was only 0.3 percent of cumulative GNP for 1973–82. This surprisingly small cumulative surplus indicates that total domestic savings were more or less equal to total domestic investments at current prices in 1973–82, and that criticism that the excess of total domestic savings over investment found an outlet in foreign countries in the form of large net exports does not hold true for Stage 3.

Two questions then arise: First, what accounts for the underlying current account surplus that emerged after the mid-1960s? Second, what is the basic feature of the sectoral SI imbalances in Stage 3, characterized by the two oil crises? How should the restoration of the current account surplus after each oil crisis be interpreted?

Generally speaking, a major cause of the persistent current account imbalance is the international difference in the marginal productivity of capital due to differences in technology, industrial mix, and capital endowment. If this is the case, a rising domestic investment ratio to GNP tends to result in current account deficits. In fact, total fixed capital formation, including public works expenditure and residential construction, increased from 20.4 percent

TABLE 4.3 JAPAN'S SAVINGS-INVESTMENT IMBALANCES, BY SECTOR, 1970–73 AND 1981–82

	Sector								Errors and omissions	
	Household		Corporate		Government		Foreign[a]			
	1970 –73	1981 –82	1970 –73	1981 –82	1970 –73	1981 –82	1970 –73	1981 –82	1970 –73	1981 –82
Savings (S)	15.8	18.0	16.3	9.7	6.8	3.4	..	..	..	..
Investment (I)	5.6	7.4	25.4	16.2	6.0	7.0	..	..	..	..
S − I	10.2	10.6	− 9.1	− 6.5	0.8	− 3.6	− 1.4	− 0.7	− 0.3	0.2

SOURCE: Economic Planning Agency 1984a.
a. New flow.

of nominal GNP in 1952 to 31.5 percent in 1967. During this Stage 1, Japan registered current account deficits, as mentioned earlier. In Stage 2 the ratio of total fixed capital formation to nominal GNP remained at a high plateau of 33 percent to 36 percent, while the savings rate in the household sector increased from 18 percent to 21 percent during the same period. These developments in both domestic investment and savings were consistent with the emergence of the current account surplus during Stage 2.

In Stage 3, the sectoral SI balance has drastically changed, reflecting a major feature of the Japanese economy in the 1970s, i.e., a sharp reduction in the underlying growth rate of real GNP from about 10 percent during Stage 2 to about 4 percent to 5 percent during Stage 3. Corresponding to the reduced underlying growth rate of real GNP, the excess of corporate investments over savings relative to GNP declined by nearly 3 percent of GNP from 1970–73 to 1981–82, while households' excess savings over investment increased somewhat relative to GNP during the same period. As a result, the private sector as a whole (corporate and household) generated excess savings. Corresponding to such newly emerged excess private savings, the general government (central, local, and the social security account) registered a deterioration in its SI balance by more than 4 percent of GNP from a surplus in 1970–73 to a relatively large deficit in 1981–82 (table 4.2). During the same period, the current account surplus declined by nearly 1 percent mainly due to the aftermath of oil deficits in the current account under the second oil shock. In other words, excess private savings, generated mainly by a decline in the GNP ratio of private expenditure on plant and equipment, have been more or less offset by the increase in the ratio of the general government deficit to GNP, without much affecting the GNP ratio of the current account surplus which had already emerged, as mentioned earlier, during Stage 2.

Despite the substantial increase in the GNP ratio of the budgetary deficit from the early 1970s to the early 1980s, there has been no indication of an acceleration of domestic inflation measured by the GNP deflator, or of crowding out of private capital formation through higher real interest rates. This is

because the general government deficit increased only to the extent of the excess private savings generated by the lower private investment ratio. Thus, the large government deficit has played two roles during Stage 3. One is to keep the Japanese economy close to high-employment output by absorbing the newly generated excess private savings. The other is to keep the current account surplus in nominal terms approximately at the same ratio to GNP after each oil shock as in Stage 2. In sum, the high-employment government deficit and high-employment current account surplus have coexisted in Stage 3, except for the periods immediately after the two oil crises.

By employing the sectoral SI balance, we can summarize as follows with regard to the existence of Japan's high-employment external surplus. During the period from the early 1970s to the early 1980s, Stage 3 in the evolution of Japan's balance of payments after World War II, Japan has become a capital exporter in terms of both flow and stock. During this stage, while the excess of household savings over investment has remained largely unchanged on the order of 10 percent of GNP, the excess of corporate investment over savings has declined from about 9 percent to 6 percent of GNP. As a result, excess savings have emerged in the private sector as a whole. The decline in the excess of corporate investment over savings has been attributed to a larger decline in investment than in savings, which corresponds to a substantial slowdown in the growth rate of real GNP from high (10 percent a year) to medium (4 percent to 5 percent annually).

Also during Stage 3, the high-employment imbalance of the general government has changed from a surplus of about 1 percent of GNP to a 3 percent deficit. In other words, new excess private savings have been absorbed by the general government deficit, whereby the high-employment current account surplus, which had already appeared in Stage 2, has reemerged after each oil crisis during Stage 3, and the Japanese economy has restored its net international creditor position. In the present Japanese economy, therefore, the high-employment current account surplus coexists with the high-employment government deficit.

POLICY PROBLEMS FACING JAPAN AS A CAPITAL EXPORTER

Given the likely continued coexistence of the high-employment government deficit and the high-employment current account surplus in Japan, new policy questions will face both the Japanese and foreign policymaking authorities. They are:

- Should domestic macroeconomic policy be aimed at reducing Japan's large current account surplus?
- How are the high-employment current account surplus and trade friction interrelated?

• How will the liberalization and internationalization of the Japanese financial market and its integration with international capital markets affect the conduct of monetary policies?

With regard to macroeconomic policy when a high-employment current account surplus exists, both foreign authorities and domestic Keynesians advocate an expansionary fiscal policy. The very existence of a current account surplus, in their view, reflects too weak a domestic demand in Japan.

This position ignores the fact that a current account imbalance can have different causes. If the exchange rates among major currencies are extremely misaligned by a criterion of the purchasing power parity for tradable goods, a large current account imbalance should emerge among major countries. For instance, Japan's large current account surpluses in 1971–72 reflected the undervalued exchange rate of the yen under the adjustable-peg Bretton Woods system. It goes without saying that exchange rates between the US dollar and other major currencies have been abnormally misaligned in recent years. Changes in prices of petroleum imports also influence currencies and the size of the current account imbalance. More importantly, the different paths various countries take to domestic adjustment to oil-price hikes greatly affect the subsequent current account development of each country. Furthermore, a country's stage of economic development and related balance of payments evolution should determine whether it is a capital importer for its development or a capital exporter based on a chronic current account surplus.

However, more relevant to macroeconomic policy are cyclical current account imbalances attributable to domestic demand conditions. They involve two issues, one domestic, the other international. On the domestic issue, cyclical and noncyclical components of the current account imbalance have to be separated. Allowing for a high-employment current account imbalance in view of an economy's stage of economic and balance of payments development, it would be inappropriate to employ only macropolicies to remove current account imbalances. Therefore, if a macroeconomic policy is selected to remove a current account imbalance, it should not attempt to eliminate the whole imbalance but just the cyclical components of the imbalance beyond or below the high-employment current account imbalance. In other words, under normal exchange rates, petroleum import prices, and international business cycles, fluctuations in domestic demand should cyclically affect the peripheral part of the current account imbalance, not the core part, i.e., the high-employment current account surplus.

In addition, the international business cycle also influences this peripheral part of the imbalance, somewhat blurring whether the current account imbalance beyond the core part is attributable to a phase of domestic demand or to the international business cycle. The best example of this is the US deficit and Japan's surplus on current account in 1984–85. Each imbalance will account for 2.5 percent to 3 percent of GNP, both excessive imbalances. A compromise policy recommendation would be to reduce the US deficit by cutting its fiscal deficit, on one hand, and to reduce Japan's surplus by expanding its government deficit on the other. Such a suggestion, however, may be risky, if the peripheral part of Japan's current account surplus is simply a counterpart of the US large current account deficit attributable to its fiscal-policy-led strong recovery.

For example, the EPA world econometric model indicates that a sustained expansionary fiscal policy in the United States equivalent to 1 percent of GNP improves Japan's current account by $2.8 billion to $5.8 billion (on current scale) in the second and third years, respectively, after its initial policy shock. If US fiscal expansion measured by the cyclically adjusted fiscal deficit is assumed to be equivalent to 2.5 percent of its GNP as stated earlier, the bulk of the peripheral part (about $15 billion) of Japan's total surplus in 1984–85 (about $30 billion) can be accounted for by the US fiscal policy. If so, for international policy coordination, Japan's fiscal policy should be expansionary, *if* and *only if* US fiscal policy becomes less expansionary, which leads us to what I call the machinery investment recession in Japan rather than just an inventory investment recession.

The EPA model also demonstrates that an expansionary fiscal policy in the United States exerts an appreciating effect on the US dollar, whereas such policy in other countries contributes to depreciations of their own currencies (Yoshitomi 1984). This great asymmetry implies that expansionary fiscal policies in non-US economies would not improve the presently misaligned exchange rates between the US dollar and other major currencies.

Hence, the existence of Japan's current account surplus does not necessarily imply that it is attributable to its weaker domestic demand and that its macro policy should be expansionary. Policymakers, domestic as well as foreign, should be obliged to judge whether the size of the existent surplus is larger or smaller than the high-employment current account surplus and what the basic causes are of the peripheral part of the current surplus.

The second question concerns the relationship between Japan's chronic current account surplus and continuing trade friction.

Theoretically, the existence of the high-employment current account surplus per se will not cause continuing trade friction between Japan and its partner countries. The existence of the chronic surplus does not mean an expanding surplus but rather a constant surplus in relation to GNP. In other words, exports and imports will grow parallel to each other on a cyclically adjusted basis. If the main cause of trade conflicts is the importation of unemployment due to trading partners' expanding deficits on current account as a counterpart of Japan's expanding surplus, then the question is not the existence of the chronic surplus but Japan's expanding net exports. In addition, such rising net exports should be measured in real terms because rising unemployment in trading-partner countries should be attributable to their lower real output due to an excess of real imports over real exports.

In fact, during all of three periods of serious trade friction (1970–72,

1977–78, 1981–1984), Japan's real exports expanded more rapidly than its real imports, but for different reasons. The bulk of the expanded net exports in real terms during 1973–82 compensated for large nominal oil deficits in the current account and restored Japan's position as a capital exporter after the oil crises. A resultant cumulative nominal surplus was small during the same period as mentioned earlier, but trade friction was serious, because net exports in real terms expanded very rapidly. It is, therefore, incorrect to say that continuing trade friction is built into Japan's high-employment current account surplus.

A related but different issue concerns trade conflicts. When a national economy grows very rapidly, its real exports will expand faster than the slow-growing domestic market of trading-partner countries. The resultant increasingly higher share of products of the fast-growing country tends to cause trade conflicts, despite the country's possibly parallel growth of exports to imports. Theoretically, however, trading-partner countries as a whole must be enjoying faster expansion in their exports to the fast-growing economies than in their own domestic market.

This issue leads to a question of how trading-partner countries can make economic adjustments to rising imports from fast-growing countries, namely, positive or negative adjustment policies. In this context, trade barriers imposed by trading partners on one sector of Japan's exports to mitigate hardship inevitably involved in such structural adjustments are bound to cause other export sectors to expand even faster to generate the high-employment current account surplus that should correspond to high-employment SI equilibrium in Japan.

A third policy problem or challenge for Japan as a capital exporter is the new way monetary and fiscal policies are conducted in the new financial environment. The Japanese financial system is shifting from the bank credit control to the open money market paradigm. This shift should change the way monetary policy is conducted in Japan, from the window guidance type of bank credit control to open market operations. The former paradigm is based on administered interest rates in the banking system and in the primary securities market, whereas in the latter paradigm, interest rates as well as issue rates are market determined. Monetary policies are targeted at the money supply, either implicitly under the bank credit control paradigm or explicitly under the open money market paradigm.

During the high-growth period, the Bank of Japan managed money supply by rationing bank credit control. Having experienced excess money supply and rapid inflation in the early 1970s, the target has been set explicitly at the money supply (M2) which is managed by combining bank credit rationing and open market operations. Once the shift to the open money market paradigm is completed through the introduction of the Treasury bill market and the related liberalization of interest rates, open market operations will become the most important instrument for money supply management.

The liberalization and internationalization of the Japanese financial system will give rise to another fundamental problem for financial policies. Can the domestic monetary policy be independent in the integrated world capital market?

The internationalization of the Japanese financial market and its consequent integration with the international capital market will make it difficult for the Bank of Japan to influence domestic real interest rates. If long-run inflationary expectations affect long-term nominal interest rates and if international differences in underlying inflationary expectations between the United States and Japan affect the expected rate of depreciation of a currency in the long run, then the expected rate of return on yen bonds tends to be equal to that on dollar bonds. This is because higher real interest rates in the United States will attract capital from Japan so long as the international difference in the expected rate of return favors dollar bonds. This relationship will hold increasingly true since the internationalization of the Japanese financial market enhances the degree of substitutability between yen and dollar bonds.[1]

If real interest rates tend to be more or less equal between home and foreign capital markets through internationalization of the Japanese financial market and through resultant integration of the two capital markets, monetary policies will not be able to influence domestic interest rates in real terms and, therefore, cannot be utilized for demand management.

CONCLUSION

The Japanese economy has become a natural international creditor through the evolution of its balance of payments, reflecting changes in the domestic sectoral SI imbalance. The unique character of the sectoral SI imbalance in Japan is the coexistence of high-employment government deficits and high-employment current account surpluses in the 1970s and 1980s. Such coexistence has accelerated the liberalization of exchange controls and financial regulations in Japan since the end of the 1970s, excluding the first oil-crisis period through sustained current account surpluses and rapid internal government debt accumulation.

The existence of Japan's high-employment current account surplus should not be a cause for trade friction between Japan and its trading partners, since it does not imply ever-growing net Japanese exports. What is important for

---

[1] For the long-term asset market equilibrium, $i = e + i^*$, where i = home nominal interest rate, i^* = dollar nominal interest rate, and e = the expected rate of appreciation of the home currency per dollar. As noted in the text, if $i = r + p$ and $i^* = r^* + p^*$ and if $e = p - p^*$, where r and r^* denote home and dollar *real* interest rates, respectively, and p and p^* denote home and US inflation rates, respectively, then the equilibrium condition for the asset market should be that $r + p = e + (r^* + p^*) = (p - p^*) + (r^* + p^*)$, that is, $r = r^*$.

countercyclical fiscal policy is the cyclical part of Japan's external imbalance over and above its core part, which is caused by weak domestic demand led, in particular, by a decline in private expenditure on plant and equipment. During the world recession in 1980–82, Japan's GNP gap remained rather small, reflecting its mild recession and continued positive growth of private expenditure on plant and equipment.

Thus, the cyclical part of Japan's current account surplus can be attributed less to weak domestic demand relative to potential output than to the expanded structural government deficit in the United States, as demonstrated by multiplier simulations of the EPA world econometric model. This EPA model has also found a great asymmetry in the impact of expansionary fiscal policies on exchange rates between the United States and the remaining major countries. US expansionary fiscal policies exert appreciating effects on the US dollar, whereas such policies in other countries contribute to depreciations of their own currencies. This asymmetry, therefore, suggests that expansionary fiscal policies in major countries other than the United States will not lead to rectifying current exchange rate misalignments, i.e., the extreme overvaluation of the US dollar, although they would reduce the large current account imbalance, particularly between the United States and Japan.

The freer international capital mobility and the more perfect the substitutability between home and US bonds, the less independent are domestic long-term interest rates in real terms from US real interest rates. Such increasingly higher dependence upon real US interest rates strongly suggests that the US policy mix should avoid too high real interest rates. Too high long-term real interest rates will be incompatible with sustainable growth of productive capacity due to possible crowding out of private expenditure on plant and equipment, possibly in countries other than the United States, because they are currently less equipped with large tax concessions to their own private fixed capital formation than is the United States. In this sense, new international macroeconomic cooperation under flexible exchange rates may be needed.

REFERENCES

ECONOMIC PLANNING AGENCY, GOVERNMENT OF JAPAN. 1983. "Re-estimation of Full Employment Government Surplus." Tokyo.
———. 1984. Annual Report on National Account.
———. 1984. The World Econometric Model. February version. Tokyo.
DE LEEUW, F., and B. P. HOLLOWAY. October 1983. "Measuring and Analysing the Cyclically Adjusted Budget." In The Economics of Large Government Deficits. Proceedings of a conference sponsored by the Federal Reserve Bank of Boston, October 1983. Melvin Village, N.H.
HOOPER, P., and R. TYRON. January 1984. "The Current Account of the US, Japan and Germany: A Cyclical Analysis." International Financial Discussion Papers, no. 236.
YOSHITOMI, MASARU, and EPA WORLD MODEL GROUP. March 1984. "The Insulation and Transmission Mechanisms of Floating Exchange Rates Analysed by the EPA World Econometric Model." Tokyo: Economic Planning Agency, Government of Japan.

Chapter 4 Discussion

Lawrence B. Krause began the discussion by noting Yoshitomi's emphasis that Japan need take no policy steps to deal with its current account problem because half the surplus was structural and the other half was due to dollar overvaluation. Krause came to a different view because he found that the model on which Yoshitomi based his analysis treated trade and exchange rate outcomes as exogenous variables. This implied that the rest of the world should accept whatever external results emerged from Japan's internal conditions, an assumption that was acceptable for a small country but not for Japan. More specifically, an assumption of "normalcy" for Japan's current external position ignored the likely unsustainability of the LDC trade deficits of 1982–83 and the stimulus to Japan's exports from US policy during the same period.

Krause suggested that Yoshitomi might even be underestimating the structural component of Japan's external surplus, which he himself would put at 3.5 percent to 4 percent of GNP. Since the world could not adjust to such a surplus, Krause said, Japan should stop its current fiscal contraction and avoid any relapse to economic stagnation. Moreover, since significant import expansion was unlikely in Japan, a key policy question was whether the structural current account surplus would be sustained by a growth in merchandise exports or by earnings from services transactions.

Juergen B. Donges noted a similarity between Yoshitomi's analysis and that of Gary R. Saxonhouse at an earlier Institute conference, suggesting that Japan's situation could be readily explained by normal economic relationships.[1] He rejected as an alibi the view that "Japan does not import," noting that German firms were losing out to Japanese firms in third countries, too. He

---

[1] Gary R. Saxonhouse, "The Micro- and Macroeconomics of Foreign Sales to Japan," in *Trade Policy in the 1980s*, edited by William R. Cline (Washington: Institute for International Economics, 1983).

suggested that Japan had adjusted to declines in its comparative advantage in particular industries, and wondered whether Europe should not emulate Japan's industrial policies.

W. Max Corden pointed out that under the structural conditions developed by Yoshitomi, an increase in Japanese imports would produce a further corresponding rise in Japanese exports and would thus generate more, not less, trouble for the world trading system. He thought that Japan was doing the world a great favor through its substantial capital exports, which hold interest rates down abroad, and that Japan's fiscal tightening was furthering this favorable effect. Corden noted that other Asian countries, contrary to Krause's fears, were adapting to Japan's competitiveness through wage moderation; he thought this might carry a lesson for Europe.

Niels Thygesen suggested, in this context, that the form of Japan's capital exports was important. Direct investment could represent an alternative to Japanese merchandise exports.

Thygesen also noted Yoshitomi's view that fiscal expansion produced a stronger currency in the United States but a weaker currency in Europe and Japan, and asked how that could be. John Williamson replied that there had been no monetary accommodation to fiscal deficits in the United States of late, whereas there had been such accommodation in most other countries. Yoshitomi suggested that the sheer size of the United States and its capital markets added to the asymmetry.

Several other specific questions were raised concerning points made by Yoshitomi. William H. Branson asked whether recent US policy had really been positive for Japan when the recession of 1981–82 was taken into account, with its adverse effects on Japanese (and other countries') exports. Jeffrey D. Sachs asked whether Japan could channel its capital exports to the developing countries, which badly needed such infusions, rather than to the United States—especially while the United States was draining capital from the rest of the world. Sachs also wondered whether the level of savings in Japan would remain as high as in recent years, noting that this was above the historical average. I. G. Patel asked whether Japan's "unofficial nontariff barriers" were cultural phenomena, and whether there had been efforts to change the situation via public education. C. Fred Bergsten wondered what implications emerged from Yoshitomi's analysis for the US current account position.

Yoshitomi replied that his model suggested a structural US current account deficit equal to about 2 percent of American GNP. As to policy, he believed that Japan should pursue fiscal expansion only if the United States decided to pursue fiscal contraction, which in turn generated a "machinery investment" (as opposed to "inventory investment") recession in Japan. He concurred that Japan should make every effort to direct its capital outflow to developing countries by increasing official aid and liberalizing the treatment of syndicated private loans.

5 Indebted Developing-Country Prospects and Macroeconomic Policies in the OECD

Mario Henrique Simonsen

In the last few years, indebted less developed countries (LDCs) have been severely struck by the escalation of dollar interest rates, by the 1981–82 recession, and by the dollar's unusual strength. The disruption of the golden transfer dynamics of the 1960s and 1970s, when LDC exports grew at rates well above international interest rates, led to the collapse of voluntary lending by commercial banks and, as a consequence, to the debt crisis. Credit rationing forced many LDCs, including most Latin American countries, to adopt tough adjustment programs supported by the International Monetary Fund (IMF) and to transfer abroad a sizable proportion of their export revenues. In fact, debtor-country policymakers now face a major puzzle, namely, to guess how much and for how long the country will need to transfer resources abroad to keep its access to foreign credit markets.

THE DOLLAR TRAP

Conventional wisdom says that debtor countries must now transfer resources abroad because they overborrowed in the late 1970s, failing to realize that, sooner or later, Organization for Economic Cooperation and Development (OECD) nations would adopt anti-inflationary policies that would raise real interest rates and bring the LDCs' export boom to a halt. If external borrowing was used to finance productive investment, dividends should now be collected to start repaying the debt, and this can be achieved with acceptable social

51

costs. If foreign loans were used to finance consumption, exchange rate overvaluation, or capital flight, LDCs should now pay for their previous attempt to live beyond their means.

What conventional wisdom overlooks is the central role of the dollar in a world of floating exchange rates, variable interest rates, and unstable rules of international trade. What has made LDCs' adjustment programs extremely painful is not the OECD countries' decision to fight inflation but the United States' choice to fight inflation with an unorthodox blend of tight monetary and loose fiscal policies—a policy mix that could hardly be successful except under the floating exchange rate regime, and which bears some similarities to some Latin American attempts to reduce inflation through exchange rate overvaluation. Were the LDCs' debts predominantly yen- or DM-denominated, instead of dollar-denominated, the developing-country debt problem would be easily solved.

This paper discusses two central issues, the dependence of the developing-country debt outlook on OECD macroeconomic policies and the adequacy of the IMF-supported adjustment programs.

What complicates the debt problem is that the visible actors—the indebted countries and their private creditors—have virtually no power to orchestrate a long-term solution. The fundamental question addressed by LDCs' policy-makers—how much and for how long their countries will need to transfer resources abroad to keep their access to foreign credit markets—cannot be answered by commercial banks in a world of floating exchange rates, variable interest rates, and unstable rules of international trade. All banks can do is stretch maturities, lower spreads, and provide additional loans to enable debtor countries to meet their interest obligations, hoping that the muddling-through strategy sponsored by the IMF and the major central banks will eventually yield a solution. Whether this solution will emerge basically depends on the OECD's macroeconomic policies. If those policies are unresponsive to the debt problem, LDC decisionmakers may turn to inward-oriented economic strategies because of risk aversion and as a hedge against adverse selection. In fact, a number of developing countries view their economic ties with the OECD as an unfair game, where the rules of play can be modified by the wealthy partners.

Another reason for concern is the absence of evidence of optimality in several IMF-supported adjustment programs, Brazil being an outstanding example. Debtor-country current account performances have improved impressively since 1982 but, under credit rationing, this may be nothing more than the display of a budget constraint. Successful adjustment should also lead to growth with relative price stability; this is the actual challenge to the competence of both the IMF and debtor-country policymakers. Policymakers are often reluctant to make explicit that adjustment requires a once-and-for-all reduction in the society's welfare, a point that is not clarified by the old-fashioned IMF conditionality model. Failure to address this question only aggravates welfare losses with wasteful stagflation.

THE TRANSFER PROBLEM

Debt dynamics can be summarized by the equation:

$$(1) \; \dot{z} = (i - x) z + g$$

where z indicates the net debt-export ratio, $\dot{z}$ its time derivative, g the resource gap-export ratio, i the average interest rate on outstanding debt, and x the growth rate of exports.[1] Net debt is to be understood as total foreign indebtedness *minus* reserves. Resource gap is defined as noninterest current account deficit, *minus* direct investment, *plus* capital exports.

Growth theories of the 1950s and 1960s accepted that capital should flow from industrial to less developed countries to improve the international allocation of resources. The assumption that the marginal productivity of capital was a decreasing function of the capital-labor ratio meant that LDCs were natural capital absorbers. Foreign capital should help developing countries expand their exports and their GNPs, creating the conditions for future profit and interest remittances. Moreover, net capital inflows could exceed profit and interest remittances as long as LDCs were able to keep their exports growing at rates above the international interest rates, yielding a positive balance of payments transfer to developing countries.

These post-Keynesian transfer models inspired most commercial bank recycling after the first oil shock (1973–74). Statistical evidence of the 1960s and 1970s suggested that LDC exports would grow at rates well above international interest rates. In fact, from 1974 through 1980, a typical interest rate on developing-country loans—London Interbank Offer Rate (LIBOR) plus 1.5 percent a year spread—averaged 10.7 percent a year while exports of nonoil LDCs expanded at 21.1 percent annually. Under the $x - i > 0$ hypothesis, lending to LDCs offered little risk. Debtors would hardly seek a confrontation with creditors as long as they were prepared to refinance all the debt service, making $g = 0$ in equation (1). And with $g = 0$ and a positive $x - i$ differential, debt-export ratios would gradually fall, bringing credit-standing ratios to any desirable level. Moreover, with export growth consistently surpassing international interest rates, a resource gap-export ratio $g = (x - i) z$ could be accommodated without raising the debt-export coefficient.

---

[1] Indicating by D the dollar net debt and by G the resource gap, $\dot{D} = i D + G$ is a balance of payments tautology. If X stands for the dollar exports, $z = D/X$ and $x = \dot{X}/X$, equation (1) is equivalent to the above-mentioned tautology.

A sudden and unanticipated change of sign in the $x - i$ differential in 1981–82 led to the debt crisis; average interest rates on commerical bank loans to LDCs soared to 16.3 percent a year, while the annual growth rate of exports declined to 1 percent. Debt-export ratios rose substantially in this two-year period, sometimes entering a dangerous zone, close to 4 for Brazil and Mexico and 5 for Argentina and Chile.

The shift from favorable to adverse debt dynamics, i.e., the change of sign of the $x - i$ differential, moved conventional wisdom on foreign lending from one pole to its opposite. William R. Cline, for example, notes:

> As was widely recognized in the mid-1970s and again in 1979–80, bank lending played a socially valuable role in facilitating the financial recycling of OPEC surpluses to nonoil developing countries in the process of adjustment. Official lending responded only sluggishly, especially to middle-income countries, so that it was primarily bank lending that met the sharply increased need for financing. Moreover, as was repeatedly pointed out at the time, if this lending had not been forthcoming, developing countries would have been forced to cut back their imports from industrial countries, causing an even sharper world recession after the first oil shock.[2]

Under the golden transfer dynamics of the 1970s this was the conventional view on lending to LDCs. Since the collapse of competitive recycling, witch hunters discuss who is responsible for the debt crisis—commercial banks that lent imprudently or developing countries that borrowed irresponsibly? But a crisis can hardly be explained by the errors of many independent actors. The central point was the change in the macroeconomic policies of the United States.

It is now largely agreed that many LDCs are overindebted and should turn equation (1) into its equivalent:

$$(2) \qquad \dot{z} = (i - x)\, z - h$$

where $h = -g$ stands for net transfers abroad as a proportion of exports. Equation (2) is often used to show that LDCs can pay off their debts, as well as the opposite. For example, in 1984 Brazil's debt-export ratio was 3.7 and it transferred abroad one-third of its export revenues. If Brazil sustains this transfer-export ratio and if the growth rate of Brazilian exports equals the average interest rate on its outstanding debt, the country can pay off its external debt in 11 years. However, the exercise is largely useless since there is no evidence that Brazil will transfer abroad for 11 years one-third of its export revenues or that the export growth rate will equal the interest rate.

What complicates the debt problem is that for both indebted countries and their private creditors equation (2) is a stochastic differential equation that

---

[2]   William R. Cline, *International Debt and the Stability of the World Economy* (Washington: Institute for International Economics, 1983), p. 94.

leaves the solvency issue in a gray zone. A key variable, the $x - i$ differential, is largely out of their control, depending on OECD macroeconomic policies. In the short run, the muddling-through strategy under the leadership of the IMF and the major central banks prevails because for most debtor countries, the social costs of an IMF-supported adjustment program are lower than the cost of a cutoff of external commercial credits, the automatic sanction imposed by commercial banks on defaulting countries. (Argentina may be an important exception.) Looking at the long term, however, several concerns arise.

First, successful adjustment policies should lead to declining debt-export ratios. In 1983 Latin America failed to meet this test despite the transfer abroad of 27.5 percent of its export revenues. Since adjustment was achieved through import reduction, the debt-export ratio of the region continued to rise, from 3.3 to 3.5 according to estimates by the Economic Commission for Latin America (ECLA). Part of this adverse result is attributed to linkage effects: import cuts in one country implied export losses in the others. However, even if statistics treat Latin America as a consolidated block, canceling intraregional trade and debts, the 1983 achievements are lackluster in terms of debt-export ratios. Results may be better in 1984, mainly because of the exceptional increase of Latin American exports to the United States. But, they are not enough to indicate a declining trend in the z ratio, especially because the present US trade deficit may be unsustainable in the next few years.

Second, unless a firm downtrend in the debt-export ratios is established, banks will be reluctant to supply additional loans to enable debtor countries to meet their interest obligations. Stated another way, in the absence of additional official lending, debtor countries would have to sustain transfer-export ratios given by $h = iz$. Under the present interest-rate outlook, this would require some large debtor countries to transfer abroad 50 percent of their export revenues, 5 percent of their GNP, or more. Transfers of such magnitude cannot be sustained for long. Debtor countries would be encouraged to adopt strong import substitution policies, to increase trade among themselves, and to dispense with international commercial credits. Eventually, a debtors' cartel might coalesce around politicians and others demanding a broad debt rescheduling, with adequate grace periods, appropriate amortization terms, and fair interest rates.

This is not to say that the debt problem is hopeless and that the muddling-through strategies can only postpone an inevitable debtor-creditor clash. OECD countries can minimize the risks of a confrontation in several ways.

First, debtor-country policymakers should perceive that OECD macroeconomic policies are responsive to the debt problem. The central question, of course, is to improve the $x - i$ differential in the debt dynamics equation, which can be achieved either by lower interest rates, reduced protectionism, or higher rates of OECD growth.

Second, debtor-country transfers abroad should be hedged against dollar interest-rate fluctuations. As an example, debtor countries would undertake to transfer abroad 9 percent a year on their outstanding debts, the difference being refinanced either through partial capitalization schemes (which would not trigger the classification of loans as nonperforming) or, preferably, through the creation of an IMF interest-rate facility. The transfer rate would be periodically reviewed (say, every three years) and should be set somewhat above the expected real dollar interest rate.

Third, adjustment policies should quickly lead to debtor-country growth. For a society with no weakness in aggregate demand, transferring abroad H billion dollars means giving up the same amount of domestic expenditures. In particular, it implies a sizable contraction of living standards and consumption outlays, if domestic savings must be raised to maintain investment levels. Yet in a growing economy with low unemployment, social tensions may be easy to dissipate. To keep developing debtor countries cooperating with the international financial community, a basic question must be addressed: under what conditions will rational policymakers in debtor nations prefer cooperation to confrontation? While precise rupture points are difficult to locate, a general principle remains valid: a growing economy with expanding exports would hardly seek confrontation with its creditors.

ADJUSTMENT AND REAL WAGES

To promote external adjustment without a real wage squeeze is the policymaker's dream. The theoretical possibility of such an achievement is illustrated by a simple two-sector model:

$$W = P_1 f_1'(N_1) = P_2 f_2'(N_2)$$

where W indicates the nominal wage, P_1 and P_2 the prices of tradable and nontradable goods, and $f_1'(N_1)$ and $f_2'(N_2)$ the marginal productivities of labor in each sector. Adjustment policies should raise the relative price P_1/P_2 of traded goods in terms of nontradables. Assuming decreasing marginal productivities and an economy kept on its production possibility frontier, part of the labor force $N = N_1 + N_2$ will be transferred from the production of nontradables to tradables. As a result, wages will decline in terms of traded goods but increase in terms of nontraded ones. The final outcome depends on marginal productivity elasticities and on the weights of traded and nontraded goods in the workers' consumption basket. However, the model opens the possibility that successful adjustment will lead to a real wage increase.

In spite of its attractiveness, the model has two major shortcomings. First, it locks in the capital stock of each sector, forcing the producers of nontradables to accept the squeeze on their quasi-rents. This may be an acceptable hypothesis in the short run. Yet in the very short run, adjustment policies hardly keep the economy on its production possibility frontier. If capital is allowed to move from one sector to the other, and if the capital-labor ratio is higher for tradables than for nontradables, adjustment will reduce wages in terms of both types of goods, according to the Stolper–Samuelson theorem.

Second, the model overlooks the fact that adjustment is usually coupled with changes in fiscal policy. In theory, the redistributive effects of a budgetary cut can operate in any direction. In most cases, however, IMF-supported programs involve indirect tax increases, subsidy cuts, and social expenditure cuts that force a reduction in real wages.

That adjustment policies involve an immediate reduction in absorption, i.e., consumption plus investment, is a tautology. Who suffers the burden of adjustment is a question of political choice, but if the economy is to be kept growing, investment should be spared as much as possible.

In other words, consumption should decline as a percentage of GNP. To complicate matters, early stages of the adjustment process do not lead to growth but to recession, partly because of the need to fight inflation, and partly because the improvement in the current account is mostly based on import cuts, either as a result of rationing or of weakened aggregate demand. Moreover, in many developing debtor countries, population expands at relatively high rates. Per capita consumption, therefore, has to decline for three reasons: the need to spur savings; recession; and population growth. In many instances an immediate fall in per capita consumption close to 10 percent occurs. How this can be achieved without massive unemployment or without a real wage reduction may be an unsolvable problem. To be sure, adjustment would involve very limited social costs if external imbalances were caused by large imports of luxury goods consumed by wealthier groups, yet this is a rather exceptional case.

Summing up, external adjustment with no real wage decrease has some similarity with Giffen goods (product for which demand decreases as income increases). It is a possibility, but a very unusual one. Some regressive fiscal reforms coupled with adjustment policies unnecessarily aggravate real wage losses, a point that is overlooked by IMF conditionality tests. Yet the failure to make explicit that adjustment may require a temporary decline in workers' living standards tends only to prolong welfare losses through wasteful stagflation.

A simple supply-side macroeconomic model highlights this point. The model is based on the following equations:

(3) $\quad P_t = W_t;$

(4) $\quad q_t = (1 - a)P_t + a(e_t + P_t'),\ (0 < a < 1);$

(5) $\quad \pi_t = q_t - q_t - 1;$

(6) $\quad \theta_t = e_t + P_t' - P_t;$

(7) $\quad w_t - w_{t-1} = (1-\beta)E_{t-1}\,\pi_t + \beta\pi_{t-1} + \gamma y_{t-1},\ (0 < \beta < 1).$

Equation (3) is a mark-up rule, where P and W stand for the logs of the GNP-implicit deflator and the nominal wage index. Equation (4) defines q, the log of the consumer price index, and e and P', indicate the nominal exchange rate and price of imported goods. Equations (5) and (6) define the inflation rate π and the real exchange rate θ. Finally, equation (7) expresses the rate of increase of nominal wages as a function of expected and past inflation rates as well as of y, the log of the ratio of real output to full employment equilibrium. E_{t-1} is the conditional expectation operator; β and $1 - \beta$ indicate the proportions of backward-looking and forward-looking responses of nominal wages to price increases, and γ is the degree of wage flexibility, in terms of responsiveness to unemployment.

Equations (3) to (7) lead to the Phillips relationship:

(8) $\gamma y_{t-1} = (1 - \beta)(I - E_{t-1})\pi_t + \beta(\theta_t - \theta_{t-1}) - \alpha(\theta_t - \theta_{t-1})$,

where I stands for the identity operator. In the absence of shocks and unanticipated policy changes, rational expectations yield perfect foresight, i.e., $I - E_{t-1} = 0$. In this case:

(9) $\gamma y_{t-1} = \beta(\theta_t - \theta_{t-1})$.

In the above-specified model, a real exchange rate devaluation, i.e., an increase in θ, immediately reduces the real wage, since from equations (3), (4), and (6):

(10) $w_t - q_t = \alpha\theta_t$.

Inflation would not accelerate nor would output experience a temporary decline if this could be achieved by a nominal wage cut. Keynes, in chapter 2 of *The General Theory of Employment, Interest, and Money*, shows how unusual is such a result, and equation (9) tells a quite different story. Let us assume that in period 0 the economy is at full employment ($y_o = 0$) with an inflation rate π_o and a real exchange rate θ_o. Adjustment policies are intended to raise the real exchange rate to $\theta_1 > \theta_0$ as of period 1, and to restore full employment with price stability as of period 2. According to equation (9), the first impact of devaluation will be an acceleration of the inflation rate to:

$\pi_1 = \pi_o + (\theta_1 - \theta_o)$.

To restore full employment with stable prices ($\pi = 0$) as of period 2, monetary and fiscal tightening in period 1 should reduce output by:

$$y_0 - y_1 = y_1 = \frac{\beta\pi_o + \alpha(\theta_1 - \theta_o)}{\tau}.$$

In the orthodox view, this temporary fall in output is nothing but the price to be paid for adjustment. Yet it may be transformed into intolerable recession by weak wage response to unemployment, i.e., low γ. A tempting method to

FIGURE 5.1   REAL WAGES UNDER INDEXATION

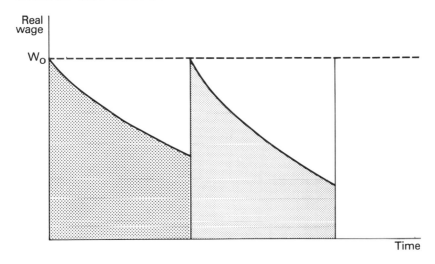

achieve adjustment without recession is to index the exchange rate so as to keep it at θ_1, in real terms, and accommodate the higher inflation rate π_1 through expansive monetary policies. As a social choice, however, this is likely to be unacceptable and certainly will not be blessed by the IMF. Faced with such adverse inflation-output trade-offs, policymakers may resort to compromises that produce nothing but prolonged stagflation.

Rigid indexation schemes are the most common source of such adverse inflation-output trade-offs. Ideal indexation arrangements would leave no room for a real wage decline, blocking any attempt to promote a real exchange rate devaluation, as shown by equation (10). In most cases, however, wage-price links involve lags through which real wages can be squeezed by an increase in inflation rates. A typical example is provided by the Brazilian indexation laws that impose nominal wage adjustments every six months, proportionally to the increase in the consumer price index.[3] The system does not actually make real wages invariant to inflation but simply restores a real wage peak W_o twice a year. The real wage curve is indicated in figure 5.1, the average real wage W_m being proportional to the shaded area which, in turn, is a decreasing function of the six-month inflation rate i. Assuming i to be uniformly distributed over time:

---

[3]   This is only an approximate description of the Brazilian wage indexation rules, since wage laws have undergone various changes since 1979. Yet it describes some of the problems created by widespread rigid indexation rules, which, in the Brazilian case, extend to several other incomes.

$$\frac{W}{m} = \frac{i}{(1 + i)\ln(1 + i)} W_o.$$

Annual inflation rates in Brazil had already escalated to 100 percent between 1980 and 1982, making $i = 0.414$ and $W_m = 0.845\,W_o$. Adjustment policies in 1983 required a 9 percent real wage reduction, as a result of a 30 percent real exchange rate devaluation, indirect tax increases, and subsidy cuts. Since indexation laws left almost no room for a reduction of W_o, the economy responded by making $W_m = 0.769 W_o$, which meant doubling the inflation rate to 200 percent a year. Real money supply has fallen more than 50 percent since early 1983, leading to explosive real interest rates and recession. Yet there are no signs that inflation is to recede from its present 200-percent-a-year rate in the near future.

IMF THEOLOGY

IMF conditionality is based on a textbook exercise inspired by the Bretton Woods tradition. An open economy with fixed exchange rates faces an infinitely elastic supply of foreign capital at a given interest rate r, but wants to reduce its external current account deficit. (It may be hard to see why such an economy would ever apply for an IMF-supported adjustment program. The implicit assumption is that IMF assistance rotates the foreign capital supply schedule by 90 degrees.) Nominal wages may be sticky, so the first step toward adjustment must be an exchange rate devaluation to make the current account target consistent with full employment. To prevent further wage increases and inflation, public sector borrowing needs must be reduced by an amount equal to the desired improvement in the external current account. With fixed exchange rates and an infinitely elastic supply of foreign capital, money supply becomes an endogenous demand-determined variable. Hence, the monetary aggregate to be tracked is net domestic credit, whose expansion leads to an equal decline in the country's foreign reserve holdings.

Some critics doubt such an economy exists. Even if it does exist, the assumption that a tax increase will reduce the current account deficit by an equivalent amount implies a marginal propensity to save equal to zero, but this is a minor detail. Since the collapse of the Bretton Woods system, fixed exchange rates are no longer the rule but the exception, and under floating exchange rates money supply is anything but an endogenous variable: net domestic assets should still be limited to prevent inflationary pressures, but money supply has nothing to do with external reserves. A crawling-peg in the Brazilian style, indexing the exchange rate to a general price index, makes the theory completely different and so on.

Despite these shortcomings, there is nothing too wrong in the demand side of the IMF conditionality model. If price stability is to be reconciled with current account improvement, an exchange rate devaluation must be combined with tight fiscal and monetary policies. Figures may be different from those established in the IMF's tests, but the general approach is valid.

The central flaws of the IMF conditionality model are to be found in the supply-side analysis. As previously remarked, there is only one departure from neoclassical macroeconomics: nominal wages are assumed to be rigid downward, so that an exchange rate devaluation may be required to reconcile external adjustment with full employment. This has two serious implications.

First, inflation-output short-term trade-offs may be quite adverse, as indicated in the previous section. When this is the case, efforts should be made to improve the Phillips relationship through adequate incomes policies to avoid prolonged and perhaps politically disruptive stagflation. Moreover, fiscal adjustment should be achieved through expenditure cuts and income tax increases. Subsidy cuts and indirect tax increases may be disastrous in highly indexed economies, not only in terms of skewed income distributions but also in terms of inflation.

Second, resumed economic growth in developing countries is crucial to resolving the debt problem. On the technical side, the requisite continued and robust LDC export growth cannot be sustained for long without real output expansion. Politically, transfers abroad by debtor countries are too heavy to be acceptable at the cost of stagnation.

Summing up, the IMF should consider prolonged economic slowdown as disturbing as galloping inflation. Especially in developing countries, it leads to social tensions and to political instability. It also yields a false balance of payments test because the current account improvement under recession may be undermined by a future recovery.

An improvement in the IMF theology would require a better balance between supply-side and demand-side analysis, besides the understanding that the world no longer lives under the Bretton Woods regime. Strict conditionality, in terms of precise short-term targets, should be limited to three points:

- balance of payments behavior
- real exchange rate levels
- reduction of protectionist measures that could harm other debtor countries' adjustment policies.

Moreover, the IMF should exact from each debtor country a comprehensive economic plan designed to fight inflation, further wage-price flexibility, strengthen domestic saving, promote export-led growth, and encourage the substitution of risk capital for external indebtedness.

DEBTOR COUNTRIES AND THE US FISCAL DEFICIT

Prospects for developing debtor countries are less dependent on their own adjustment efforts than on OECD macroeconomic policies, especially on the future of dollar interest rates and on the position of the dollar vis-à-vis other major currencies. The dollar plays a unique role in the international monetary system, and the largest part of developing-country debt is dollar-denominated. In recent years dollar appreciation due to high US interest rates, a typical byproduct of the floating exchange rate regime, made life extremely difficult for LDCs. High interest rates increased the debt-service burden, whereas the overvalued dollar depressed commodity prices, worsening LDCs' terms of trade. The only compensation for indebted LDCs was that the strong dollar coupled with the US fiscal-led recovery helped their export growth. Yet increasing exports to meet additional interest obligations is far from being a convincing welfare prescription; rather it looks like being allowed to work overtime to pay additional taxes. Moreover, the strong dollar appears to have depressed LDCs' exports to Europe and Japan.

The reasons for the dollar's strength and for the high dollar interest rates need no further diagnosis. They were caused by the unprecedented fiscal deficits in the United States, which, in turn, led to huge trade and current account deficits in the leading world economy. Part of the present capital flows to the United States, the counterpart of the country's current account deficit, can be explained by the safe-haven theory. Yet what makes this explanation largely unconvincing is why the United States must keep interest-rate differentials so high to attract foreign savings and why most of its current account deficit is financed by short-term rather than by long-term capital movements.

These remarks support the view that a strong budgetary deficit cut in the United States would be the best remedy for the developing-country debt problem. Interest rates would fall, helping to solve the transfer problem. The dollar would depreciate, improving LDCs' terms of trade and easing their exports to Western Europe and Japan, offsetting lower import demand from the United States.

This is likely to be the ideal scenario from the intermediate- and long-run perspectives, but doubts may arise about the short-run benefits of a US fiscal cut. Little is known about the short-term effects of changes in policy mixes under floating rate regimes. Theoretical models are easy to develop, but whether they stand as mere academic speculation or as accurate descriptions of exchange rate market psychology is unresolved. Most theoretical models describe different currency-denominated assets as perfect substitutes. Were this the case, high-interest-rate currencies should be depreciating, not appreciating, as is the dollar, except if expectations were continuously frustrated by shocks. Such shocks are not easy to identify, so the best explanation is that the dollar is paying a risk premium because of the poor US current account performance.

How a budget deficit cut should affect the dollar risk premium is an open question. A favorable hypothesis would be a quick fall in interest rates accompanied by a mildly depreciating dollar. This outcome would help developing debtor countries to lower their transfers abroad without losing their export revenues, which could be gradually shifted from the United States to other OECD nations. The scenario would still be improved if the Federal Reserve decided to expand the real money supply as a once-and-for-all compensation for a fiscal cut, realizing that a decline in nominal interest rates increases the demand for money.

In practice, such a fine-tuning is not likely to occur, partly because the Federal Reserve may fear a reignition of inflationary expectations, partly because exchange rate depreciation increases the prices of traded goods with an immediate impact on price indexes. Moreover, whether a US budgetary cut will overshoot or undershoot the dollar cannot be determined, since market psychology is largely unknown. This may require central bank intervention in the foreign exchange markets, not leaning into the wind, but to dampen short-term fluctuations.

A cautionary note should be added. If the present US policy mix (tight monetary and loose fiscal policies, leading to increasing current account deficits) is continued, there is a risk that some day the dollar will collapse because of a sudden change in exchange rate market psychology. The danger does not seem imminent but might emerge in the coming years. This would usher in the worst of all worlds. Dollar interest rates would explode as a consequence of the expectational move against the dollar and of the need to tighten monetary policy so as to deter inflationary pressures from both the demand and cost sides. Europe and Japan would have no time to respond to a sudden currency appreciation with accelerated growth because this would require an abrupt shift from export-led to domestic market-induced economic expansion. The result for LDCs would be a second debt shock, leading perhaps to plain insolvency.

INTEREST RATES AND THE INCOME TAX WEDGE

An important and often neglected issue is the income tax wedge built into debtor-country borrowing interest rates. Economic literature has shown that in a closed economy, a proportional income tax on interest-rate revenues has no real effect, as long as interest liabilities are treated as deductible expenditures at the same tax rates. In fact, because for lenders and borrowers the after-tax and not the pretax interest rate matters, market forces determine the after-tax rate and not the latter. Hence, if a 50 percent income tax is levied on profits and other net incomes, pretax interest rates will double without any dollar being accrued to government tax revenues. What the Treasury collects from lenders is transferred to borrowers, so that the net interest rate remains the same while the gross interest rate is adjusted to accommodate the fiscal transfer. To increase fiscal revenues, tax rates should be higher for lenders than for borrowers, but this may involve some legal complications, since today's creditor may become tomorrow's debtor.

Income tax laws in the United States (unlike those of Japan) broadly treat interest payments as lenders' taxable incomes and as borrowers' deductible expenditures, introducing a substantial gap between the pretax and after-tax rates. Incidentally, this explains why the recent US recovery has been so strong despite the abnormally high real interest rates: real interest rates are extremely high on a pretax basis, but not on a net after-tax basis. Because there is no mechanism to make balance of payment tax transfers, debtor countries must pay the pretax, not the market-determined after-tax interest rates. Moving from legal formalities to substance, this means the LDCs not only transfer net resources to help finance the US trade deficit but also, through an indirect and subtle mechanism, pay income taxes to the United States.

The logic of the income tax wedge argument is too strong to neglect. It leads to the conclusion that, ideally, all international lending should be conveyed through income-tax-free capital market instruments. But this may be too radical a proposal for the creditor-country taxpayer. A more moderate suggestion is that worldwide income-tax-free bonds would be issued only by the IMF, the World Bank, and a few other selected international lending agencies. The outstanding amounts should be controlled to keep the average interest rates paid by developing debtor countries at solvency levels. An alternative proposal with practically the same result would be additional capital contributions, from creditor countries to official lending agencies, to compensate for the fiscal transfer caused by the income tax effects on international interest rates. Incidentally, it provides a rationale for creating an interest facility at the IMF under the previously discussed terms.

6 Poor Countries and the Global Economy: Crisis and Adjustment

Deepak Lal

The international economic environment impinges on any economy via prices and terms of access to markets for—and supplies of—traded goods, services, and factors of production, including the supply of capital. In 1974–75 a deterioration of opportunities to trade in goods and services was offset for many developing countries by an improvement in opportunities for workers to migrate to the Middle East and for capital imports based on the recycling of the large financial surpluses of the oil producers. Between 1979 and 1983, in contrast, most developing countries initially—and virtually all ultimately—faced an unanticipated deterioration in every significant aspect of the economic environment (table 6.1).

Weak demand in the industrial countries from 1980 to 1983 was the main cause of declining prices of exports from developing countries (table 6.2). Industrial raw material prices fell for the additional reason that high interest rates discouraged storage, while food prices dropped because of bumper world harvests. Overall, the prices of primary goods reached a record low for the postwar period relative to prices of manufactures in 1982. By 1983, however, the recession began to give way to recovery, and supply was limited by both

This paper is based on the paper by Lal and Martin Wolf, "Debt, Deficits and Distortions: Problems of the Global Economy," on which Part 1 of the World Development Report 1984 was based. The views expressed herein are those of the authors and should not be attributed to the World Bank or to its affiliated organizations.

TABLE 6.1 POPULATION, GDP, AND GDP PER CAPITA IN 1980, AND GROWTH RATES, 1960–83

Country group	1980 GDP (billion dollars)	1980 population (millions)	1980 GDP per capita (dollars)
Developing countries[b]	2,118	3,280	650
Low-income	549	2,175	250
Asia	497	1,971	250
China	284	980	290
India	162	675	240
Africa	52	204	250
Middle-income oil importers	915	611	1,500
East Asia and Pacific	204	183	1,110
Middle East and North Africa	28	35	800
Sub-Saharan Africa[c]	37	60	610
Southern Europe	201	91	2,210
Latin America and Caribbean	445	241	1,840
Middle-income oil exporters[d]	654	494	1,320
High-income oil exporters	228	16	14,250
Industrial market economies	7,463	715	10,440

n.a. Not available.
Source: World Bank, World Development Report—1984, Washington.
a. Estimated.
b. Data for 1982 and 1983 are based on a sample of 90 developing countries.
c. Does not include South Africa.
d. The estimated 1983 data exclude Angola, Iran, and Iraq.

TABLE 6.2 CHANGES IN EXPORT PRICES AND TERMS OF TRADE, 1965–83
(average annual percentage change)

Country group	1965–73	1973–80	1981	1982	1983[a]
	Change in export prices				
Developing countries					
Food	6.6	7.8	−16.1	−14.1	5.2
Nonfood	3.7	10.1	−14.6	−9.4	10.3
Metals and minerals	1.6	5.6	−12.0	−8.0	−2.2
Fuels	6.7	24.7	10.5	−2.6	−14.5
Industrial countries					
Manufactures	4.7	10.9	−4.2	−1.8	−3.2
	Change in terms of trade				
Low-income Asia	−0.5	−1.4	−0.1	−1.6	−0.6
Low-income Africa	−0.1	−1.5	−9.9	−0.9	4.6
Middle-income oil importers	−0.6	−2.2	−5.5	−1.9	3.0
Middle-income oil exporters	1.1	8.1	9.0	−0.4	−7.0
Developing countries	0.4	1.6	−0.5	−1.2	−0.6

Note: Calculations are based on a sample of 90 developing countries.
Source: World Development Report—1984.
a. Estimated.

	GDP growth rates (average annual percentage change)				
1960–73	1973–79	1980	1981	1982	1983[a]
6.3	5.2	2.5	2.4	1.9	1.0
5.6	4.8	5.9	4.8	5.2	4.7
5.9	5.2	6.3	5.2	5.6	5.1
8.5	5.7	6.1	4.8	7.3	5.1
3.6	4.3	6.9	5.7	2.9	5.4
3.5	2.1	1.3	1.2	0.5	− 0.1
6.3	5.6	4.3	0.9	0.7	0.3
8.2	8.6	3.6	6.7	4.2	6.4
5.2	3.0	4.2	− 2.4	5.5	2.0
5.6	3.7	5.5	3.9	1.1	0.3
6.7	5.0	1.5	2.3	0.7	− 0.9
5.6	5.0	5.8	− 2.3	− 0.4	− 2.2
6.9	4.9	− 2.4	2.4	0.9	− 1.7
10.7	7.7	7.4	0.0	n.a.	n.a.
4.9	2.8	1.3	1.3	− 0.5	2.3

unfavorable weather and government policies; consequently, the prices of primary goods started to rise again. Nevertheless, prices remained low relative to those in better times and almost all developing countries faced worse terms of trade in 1983 than in 1980 (table 6.2).

As to exports from the developing countries (table 6.3), raw material and fuel quantities fell absolutely during the recession, while food exports—always relatively insensitive to income—continued to grow. Perhaps most dramatic was the decline in the growth rate of developing countries' manufactured exports, from 10.6 percent a year between 1973 and 1980 to only 6.9 percent between 1980 and 1983. Given that GDP growth rates in industrial countries were very low, however, it is clear that penetration of their markets for manufactures by developing countries must have continued despite the recession.

While extremely difficult to disentangle, it appears that low growth of income in the industrial countries rather than increased protection was the main immediate cause of deteriorating trade opportunities. This does not rule out the possibility that the costs of protection, subsidization, and other forms of resistance to change as well as uncertainty about future policies were important among the causes of slow growth in industrial countries, and that the 1980–83 recession was more protracted than previous recessions because of existing protection and associated rigidities in their economic structures. Pressures for further protection were strong but governments were for the most part able to resist them. New protectionist actions and agreements largely concerned trade among industrial countries, especially imports into Europe and North America from Japan. Moreover, several other developments adversely

TABLE 6.3 EXPORTS FROM DEVELOPING COUNTRIES, 1965–83

Commodity and developing-country group	Change in export volumes (average annual percentage change)					Value of exports (billion current dollars)	
	1965– 73	1973– 80	1981	1982	1983ᵃ	1965	1981
Commodity							
Manufactures	14.9	10.6	16.3	−1.6	6.0	7.1	134.6
Food	1.3	6.0	19.7	5.0	0.9	13.3	74.8
Nonfood	3.7	1.5	2.5	−6.1	1.7	5.4	24.5
Metals and minerals	6.3	5.9	2.6	−2.1	−1.9	4.5	26.9
Fuels	6.4	−1.3	−21.9	5.1	6.1	7.3	165.1
Developing-country group							
Low-income Asia	2.9	7.6	17.2	−3.8	4.6	5.2	36.0
Low-income Africa	4.0	−1.3	−2.6	10.6	0.2	1.9	6.6
Middle-income oil importers	8.1	7.6	12.5	−0.5	3.2	18.5	219.0
Middle-income oil exporters	5.7	−0.8	−17.0	5.2	5.7	12.0	150.5
All developing countries	6.3	3.1	0.4	1.1	4.1	37.5	412.1

Note: Data for 1982 and 1983 are based on a sample of 90 developing countries.
Source: World Development Report—1984.
a. Estimated.

affected developing countries, including a more restrictive renegotiation of the Multi-Fiber Arrangement in 1981 and subsequent restrictions on textiles and clothing (especially in the United States); further development toward comprehensive restrictions on steel imports into the United States and the European Community; and increased resort to less-than-fair-value provisions of US trade law.

As two-thirds of developing-country indebtedness was in the form of dollar-denominated debt, the sharp rise in real interest rates represented a fundamental change in their economic environment. This rise greatly increased the costs of borrowing and thereby postponing domestic adjustment, compared with the opportunities available during the 1974–75 recession. Indeed, postponing adjustment of real expenditure levels and real exchange rates, while so many countries experienced a sharp deterioration in the terms of trade, could have been justified only if the high cost of borrowing and the recession itself had turned out to be of brief duration. Unfortunately, they did not.

Because of the failure to anticipate the significance of the change in the environment, the impact of the recession on developing countries came in two distinct phases. The first—a period during which adjustment was postponed by many developing countries—ended in mid-1982; the second—a period of rapid, dramatic, and extremely painful adjustment for some developing countries—has continued since that time but may now be ending. Oil-importing countries had hoped that the shock would be brief while oil-exporting countries

TABLE 6.4 CURRENT ACCOUNT BALANCES AND THEIR FINANCING, 1970–83
(billion current dollars)

Country group and item	1970	1980	1981	1982	1983[a]
Developing countries					
Net exports of goods and nonfactor services	−9.8	−55.2	−80.5	−57.1	−10.9
Net factor income	−3.6	−16.4	−30.0	−43.2	−48.3
Interest payments on medium- and long-term loans	−2.7	−32.7	−41.2	−48.4	−49.0
Current account (excludes official transfers)[b]	−12.7	−69.6	−107.8	−97.6	−56.2
Financing					
Official transfers	2.4	11.6	11.7	10.8	11.1
Medium- and long-term loans					
Official	3.7	21.5	21.2	21.4	17.6
Private	4.6	35.7	49.6	33.5	39.9
Oil importers					
Net exports of goods and nonfactor services	−8.9	−69.3	−70.5	−46.9	−26.0
Net factor income	−1.5	−4.3	−14.4	−21.8	−23.0
Interest payments on medium- and long-term loans	−2.0	−21.3	−26.7	−31.7	−32.3
Current account (excludes official transfers)	−9.8	−70.3	−81.8	−65.6	−46.1
Financing					
Official transfers	1.8	9.6	9.4	9.0	8.9
Medium- and long-term loans					
Official	2.9	16.9	16.5	15.9	13.9
Private	3.7	24.6	30.8	22.0	11.1
Oil exporters					
Net exports of goods and nonfactor services	−0.9	14.2	−10.0	−10.1	15.1
Net factor income	−2.1	−12.1	−15.6	−21.4	−25.3
Interest payments on medium- and long-term loans	−0.7	−11.5	−14.5	−16.7	−16.7
Current account (excludes official transfers)	−2.9	1.7	−26.1	−32.1	−10.0
Financing					
Official transfers	0.6	2.2	2.3	1.8	2.2
Medium- and long-term loans					
Official	0.8	4.6	4.7	5.5	3.6
Private	0.9	11.1	18.8	11.6	28.9

Note: Calculations are based on a sample of 90 developing countries.
Source: World Development Report—1984.
a. Estimated.
b. Current account does not equal net exports plus net factor income due to omission of private transfers. Financing does not equal current account because of omission of direct foreign investment, other capital, and changes in reserves.

had not expected an adverse shock at all. By 1982 it had become evident that both groups had been wrong.

ARRIVAL OF THE "DEBT CRISIS"

Oil-importing developing countries as a group were forced to make some adjustments in the real level of their imports from the beginning of the recession.

TABLE 6.5 DEBT INDICATORS FOR DEVELOPING COUNTRIES, 1970–83
(percentage)

Indicators	1970	1974	1975	1976	1977
Ratio of debt to GNP	13.3	14.0	15.4	16.6	18.1
Ratio of debt to exports	99.4	63.7	76.4	79.6	84.7
Debt service ratio[b]	13.5	9.5	11.1	10.9	12.1
Ratio of interest service to GNP	0.5	0.7	0.8	0.8	0.9
Total debt outstanding and disbursed (billions of dollars)	68.4	141.0	168.6	203.8	249.8
Official	33.5	61.2	71.6	83.5	99.8
Private	34.9	79.8	96.9	120.3	150.0

Note: Calculations are based on a sample of 90 developing countries.
Source: World Development Report—1984.
a. Estimated.
b. Ratio of interest payments plus amortization to exports.

Nevertheless, the adjustment was far from complete. The combined current account deficits of oil-importing developing countries appear to have grown from nearly $29 billion in 1978 to $70 billion in 1980 and nearly $82 billion at their peak in 1981 (table 6.4).

Despite growing current account deficits, the huge increase in interest payments caused a squeeze on imports in oil-importing developing countries up to 1982. In that year, interest due from all developing countries, including interest on short-term debt, was $66 billion ($48 billion on medium- and long-term debt) and this accounted for approximately one-half of the total developing country current account deficit (tables 6.4 and 6.5). Nevertheless, in the aggregate, lenders were capitalizing interest for oil-importing developing countries and, in addition, making loans sufficient to cover a substantial real resource gap—that is, deficit on goods and nonfactor services—as well.

For oil-exporting developing countries the experience in the early part of the recession was markedly different from that of oil-importing developing countries, although the denouement turned out to be similar. In 1979 and 1980 oil-exporting developing countries had both current account surpluses and increased levels of real imports. The rise in the real price of oil was not sustained, however, and the value of oil exports fell. In consequence, in 1981 they too slipped into deficit—$26 billion followed by $32 billion in 1982 (table 6.4). In both years the oil-exporting countries drew down reserves, as did the oil-importing countries.

Thus, by 1982, starting from very different points of origin, both oil-importing and oil-exporting developing countries had reached a similar impasse. To understand what then happened, circumstances have to be considered under which lenders will capitalize interest payments and provide additional lending. "Credit" derives from a Latin word meaning "to believe." This question is, therefore, equivalent to asking what determines the lenders' faith in the ability or willingness of debtors to service debt out of their own income (rather than out of additional borrowing) if necessary.

1978	1979	1980	1981	1982	1983[a]
19.3	19.5	19.2	21.9	24.9	26.7
92.9	83.7	76.1	90.8	108.7	121.4
15.4	15.0	13.6	16.6	19.9	20.7
1.0	1.3	1.5	1.9	2.2	2.2
311.7	368.8	424.8	482.6	538.0	595.8
120.1	136.0	157.5	172.3	190.9	208.5
191.6	232.8	267.3	310.3	347.1	387.3

Concern about creditworthiness is related both to the *likelihood* that service of debt out of income will become necessary and to the *cost* of debt service. That cost depends on the ratio of debt to wealth (in the case of a country the present value of future national income), on the real rate of interest, on the ease with which the necessary adjustments to expenditures in relation to output can be made, and—in the case of external debt—on the cost of making external transfers. The situation was deteriorating in almost all these respects in many developing countries. Table 6.5 shows that between 1979 and 1982 ratios of debt to GNP had risen from 19.5 percent to 24.9 percent, of debt to exports from 84 percent to 109 percent, and of debt service to exports from 15 percent to 20 percent. In effect, without some adjustment, debt was on an explosive path and sooner or later lenders were bound to want to see this growth contained.

If any single event can be isolated as the turning point in the lenders' attitude, it probably occurred in August 1982 when Mexico got into difficulties over its service obligations. In the context of a debt structure with short maturities, high nominal interest rates, and a high nominal and still higher real rate of required refinance these difficulties quickly spread elsewhere. Because of the number of lenders involved, the immediate resolution involved intense activity by the monetary authorities of the industrial countries and far more involuntary lending than was desirable for a stable solution.

ADJUSTMENT IN DEVELOPING COUNTRIES

It is customary to focus on the external adjustment since it is evident that adjustment to deteriorating terms of trade, high real rates of interest, and a decline in opportunities to borrow must involve a reduction in the external resource gap in real terms. If this reduction is to be achieved, however, internal adjustment must first occur, i.e., real expenditures must be reduced in relation to real output.

In most developing countries, these internal adjustments had to start with the public sector. When countries were attempting to maintain real expenditures despite a decline in the real value of national income, they obviously had to borrow. The principal borrower was the public sector. (Even where it was not the only borrower, the importance of government as the third party in any contract, but especially one involving a commitment to make service payments in foreign exchange, led lenders to seek government guarantees.) The internal counterpart of external borrowing and the accumulation of external debt was a rise in public sector deficits. By 1982 in a number of developing countries, public sector deficits had reached 10 percent, in certain cases even as much as 15 percent, of GNP. Moreover, in the context of undeveloped domestic capital markets, such deficits could be financed even in the short term only by inflation or by borrowing abroad.

The foreign indebtedness of concern is largely that of the public sector. It may exceed a country's overall foreign indebtedness if the private sector holds foreign assets. That some developing countries are experiencing private capital flight can be inferred from the fact that their stock of international debt outstanding exceeds the sum of measured current account deficits. In this case the likely explanation is that unmeasured capital outflow has occurred. The government of such a country is, however, unable to use these private resources to meet its own liabilities and, indeed, not only the import and exchange controls but also the increased taxation frequently employed to deal with the balance of payments make it still less likely that the private outflow will be reversed.

In 1982 the decline in lending to developing countries was very marked: total private loans fell from about $56 billion in 1981 to about $29 billion in 1982; most of the drop occurred in the second half of the year. In the first quarter of 1983 private lending was only $3.3 billion, most of it involuntary lending under International Monetary Fund (IMF) rescheduling agreements. Thus the increase in medium- and long-term private lending shown in table 6.5 for 1983 or 1982 is almost entirely due to the rescheduling of existing short-term debt.

On the internal side the required adjustments to this sharp decline in lending have taken two forms: an overt attempt to reduce the size of the public sector deficit and a de facto increase in taxation through a rise in the inflation tax. Indeed, the acceleration in inflation that has occurred in a number of the principal debtor countries is not an accident. It is one important way that existing public sector deficits could be financed in the context of the decline in foreign lending. Closing the deficits by increased taxation (whether overt or covert) has often led to a marked squeeze on the private sector with serious consequences for long-term investment and growth. The same adverse effects on long-term growth must occur when public sector investment is cut, and the public sector generally finds it easier to cut investment than consumption.

Given a large enough reduction in real expenditures, the current account of the balance of payments is bound to improve. Experience shows that there are, however, more and less wasteful ways of achieving this result. In the present situation, for instance in the Southern Cone countries of Latin America, the more wasteful ways are frequently being employed. The problem is that adjustment requires a reduction of expenditures in relation to output while reductions in output themselves contribute nothing to adjustment and represent pure waste. Unfortunately, however, a rapid compression of expenditures is bound to bring about large reductions in output and, as a result, the attempt to reduce expenditures in relation to output also creates a wasteful recession.

A less costly adjustment involves switching output from the domestic toward international markets and toward import substitution while switching consumption in the opposite direction. This adjustment usually requires a real exchange rate depreciation. The process of switching is less costly if it does not occur too swiftly, if a large proportion of domestic output is easily tradable— i.e., domestic and international prices are reasonably closely aligned—and if it is easy to expand exports rather than necessary to compress imports. Many of the principal indebted countries got into trouble just because these conditions did not exist in 1982: exchange rates were seriously overvalued; economies were highly protected, often by import controls that made the protected goods effectively nontradable; and export sectors were relatively undeveloped and, in addition, faced growing external restraints. It was these very conditions and implied economic waste, combined with large current account deficits, that had made lenders nervous in the first place.

Since 1982 many developing countries have sharply reduced real expenditures and substantially improved their external accounts. For oil-importing developing countries the current account deficit (excluding official transfers) fell from $82 billion in 1981 to $66 billion in 1982 and to expected levels of $46 billion in 1983 and $49 billion in 1984 (table 6.4). For oil-exporting developing countries the deficit fell from $32 billion in 1982 to expected levels of $10 billion in 1983 and 1984. Indeed, the combined deficit in 1983 was only a little larger than the interest due in that year.

These improvements in the current account appear to have been largely the result of the compression of imports in relation to output and recession-induced reductions in demand for imports. Export promotion has not been an important part of the immediate adjustment process, which has, therefore, brought about serious domestic recession and associated waste. Thus, in the major "debt crisis" countries, imports were compressed in real terms by about half in Argentina between 1981 and 1982, by about 40 percent in Mexico between 1981 and 1982, by 30 percent in Venezuela between 1982 and 1983, and progressively by about 33 percent in Brazil between 1980 and 1983. In contrast, the real value of exports declined in Argentina and Venezuela during this period and was stagnant in Brazil. Furthermore, the import restrictions used by many indebted countries to curb imports threaten a long-term deterioration in the efficiency of trade regimes and consequent further waste in the future. Other indebted countries, Korea and Turkey, for example, have followed more appropriate adjustment policies and have succeeded in expanding both their real imports and exports during the 1980s.

One of the most important consequences of import reductions by developing countries is their recessionary impact on the world economy as a whole. Developing countries are more important markets for the European Community, the United States, or Japan individually than either of the other two. They are also of great importance to one another. This interdependence is a particularly serious problem in Latin American countries, where a long history of import substitution and schemes for regional trade integration have led to significant trade with one another—especially in manufactures. For Brazil, for example, import reductions by the rest of Latin America and also by other developing countries have seriously impaired export opportunities. Consequently, the required external adjustments are more difficult and the corresponding internal adjustments more painful than if Brazil had promoted exports to other parts of the world.

PROBLEMS AND OPPORTUNITIES FOR DEVELOPING COUNTRIES

The availability of resources and the efficiency with which they are utilized are and will remain the major determinants of developing-country performance. Many developing countries apart from sub-Saharan Africa have succeeded in raising their domestic savings to maintain sufficient growth momentum. But, given that potential returns to investment remain high, and the accompanying income increases are necessary to redress the poverty of their populations, they still need inflows of foreign capital to supplement domestic savings. To the extent that the current debt crisis has involved a capital outflow from some of the "crisis" debtors, it is important that the debt crisis is resolved so that normal flows to them can be resumed.

The problem of resource availability is particularly acute for low-income Africa, given the decline in their domestic savings rates *and* in capital inflows. Restoring domestic savings rates once again requires domestic policy reforms in these countries. But even if these savings rates were to recover to their 1970 level, the African countries would still need greater capital inflows to supplement domestic savings than most other areas of the developing world. Moreover, to the extent that one of the essential preconditions for improving the absorptive capacity for investment is the provision of physical and social infrastructure, a large part of investment will have to go into projects that have relatively long gestation lags, whose outputs are not tradable and often not even marketable. Hence, commercial private financing of such investments is unrealistic, and the public sector must finance much of this infrastructure, which poses a serious fiscal problem in most of sub-Saharan Africa. Although more can be done to raise domestic resources through more efficient tax systems, tax revenues will not likely meet the infrastructural needs of much of sub-Saharan Africa in the near future. In this context the recent decline in capital flows to the region, particularly concessional flows, is lamentable.

Sustained concessional flows are also required in sub-Saharan Africa to enable necessary domestic policy reforms, now to some extent being instituted, to have their beneficial effects on the structure of these economies—on output, the budget, and on the balance of payments—over a number of years. Given their limited ability to service commercial debt, which is in part due to their past failure to change their domestic economic and, particularly export, structures, much of the capital flow will have to be on concessional terms. It is vital, therefore, if the dismal prospects of this region are to be reversed, that official flows should expand rather than diminish in real terms, as in the past few years.

This said, in both sub-Saharan Africa and the crisis debtor countries, both major problems and opportunities are related to resource utilization inefficiencies caused by policy-induced distortions in the price mechanism. The World Bank's report *Accelerated Development in Sub-Saharan Africa* (Washington, 1981) characterized the region's crisis as a production crisis, caused by the widespread adoption of price and income structures that have provided inappropriate production incentives. In particular, the inefficient incentives to agricultural production, the creation of costly and inefficient agricultural marketing systems for both inputs and outputs, and the maintenance of overvalued effective exchange rates were identified as major policy-induced distortions in these economies. Domestic policy reform, therefore, has a high payoff for these countries, as it will allow significant increases in production despite their overall constraints on resource availability, technology, and the existing skills of their peoples.

While more efficient pricing policies in agriculture and foreign trade are thus essential for Africa, recent moves in this direction have been insufficient. Despite the need to keep effective exchange rates at internationally competitive levels, which in view of their balance of payments problems requires effective depreciation, most African countries have not devalued their effective exchange rates and have tried to close their trade deficits by cutting imports. This not only worsens the bias against exports indirectly but also leads to a much larger cut in domestic output than a more efficient adjustment to external shocks would entail.

The same conclusion applies to the insufficient changes in pricing policies, particularly those in agriculture. Although nominal producer prices have been increased in many cases, they have been lower in real terms (i.e., deflated by the farmers' cost of living) in 1982 than in 1980 in Kenya, Madagascar,

Tanzania, and Togo. In some other countries—Burkina Faso (Upper Volta), Burundi, Ivory Coast, Liberia, Mali, Malawi, Niger, and Nigeria—while the prices of a few agricultural commodities have been raised, those for many others have fallen in real terms.

The continuing problem of fiscal deficits in sub-Saharan Africa requires efforts to boost domestic revenue to improve efficiency in the allocation of the available budgetary resources. This requires greater attention to the proper evaluation and programming of public expenditures, which appears to be happening in countries such as Ivory Coast, Liberia, Madagascar, Senegal, Sudan, and Togo. But in others, like Burundi, Guinea, Mali, Malawi, and Sierra Leone, public expenditure has increased despite budgetary constraints.

Similar problems of insufficient adjustments in the crucial relative prices in the economy, which determine the efficiency of its use of resources, are also to be found in many other areas of the developing world. Thus even a country like Korea, which followed relatively efficient domestic policies for most of the 1970s and achieved rapid and uninterrupted growth through most of this period, found that its policy-induced shift toward import-substituting heavy industry was inefficient. GNP declined for the first time in 1980, inflation approached 30 percent, and the real appreciation of the exchange rate dampened export growth, leading to a current account deficit of more than 9 percent of GNP. The recent reversal of these policies suggests that these policy-induced distortions will be reduced in the near future.

The performance of developing countries in the turbulent 1970s suggests that these domestic problems of maintaining efficient incentive structures through appropriate pricing remain of great importance. Moreover, their varied experience during the past decade also underlines the importance of flexibility in their economies and public budgets. This flexibility is particularly required to reduce the losses of income and output in the face of adverse shocks. Most important of all, unsustainable public expenditure commitments based on temporarily favorable conditions must not be made, because they are difficult to reverse and the ensuing public sector deficits exacerbate the problems of domestic inflation and the maintenance of internationally competitive effective exchange rates.

Chapters 5 and 6 Discussion

Bela Balassa expressed widespread agreement with the papers—particularly regarding desirable adjustment approaches and the need to avoid counterproductive tax increases. His own research strongly supported the efficacy of outward-oriented adjustment policies in raising output, whereas inward-looking countries had simply borrowed more abroad to offset their failures to expand production. In 1983, outward-oriented countries (with a combined net debt-export ratio of 58 percent) had experienced growth of 5 percent while the latter type (with a combined ratio of 190 percent) had zero growth. Turkey, for example, achieved a dramatic expansion in its exports—despite an overall decline in the industrial world's imports—by opening its economy and basing its policies on market forces.

Balassa doubted that the "theology of the International Monetary Fund" (IMF) would change, despite policy statements supporting "supply-side" approaches. It was thus desirable for the World Bank to play a more active role, particularly through lending for structural adjustment. He supported, for insurance reasons, the proposal for a new IMF facility to provide compensatory finance against any renewed rise in interest rates.

Focusing on the situation in sub-Saharan Africa, Amir H. Jamal stressed the inadequacy of current efforts by the international financial institutions. Their emphasis on "rationalizing prices" could not guarantee increased output and often produced only higher inflation. The minimum level of needed resources was often not available, and data inadequacies compounded the difficulties. Jamal agreed with Simonsen's conclusions, although the African countries were "vastly different" from those in Latin America; he thought the IMF was "even more amiss" in Africa, and that its approach was "totally unrealistic" and would be "proven wrong over the next 10 years."

Jamal preferred a more gradual approach to the needed adjustments, aimed at increasing efficiency and reducing external dependency. Financial and structural problems were intertwined and could not be treated separately. Foreign private investment should be increased and advice to that end was well taken; however, little such investment was occurring, even for countries that were "good boys," as the firms wanted too many guarantees and the countries could not afford to expand consumption as the firms preferred.

Manea Manescu proposed a series of specific measures to help deal with the problems of the developing countries. His list included a reduction in trade barriers in the industrial countries, lower interest rates, cancellation of the external debts of the poorest countries and reduction in the debts of other less developed countries (LDCs), long-term rescheduling of the remaining debt at low or zero interest rates, a ceiling on annual debt repayments at 10 percent to 15 percent of export earnings, interest ceilings of 7 percent to 8 percent on "rescheduled" existing credits and 5 percent on new credits (0 percent to 3 percent for the least developed), steps to ensure remunerative commodity prices to producing countries, increases in the level and quality of foreign assistance (financed, along with other economic measures, by reductions of 10 percent to 15 percent in military expenditures) and expanded scientific and technological cooperation between industrial and developing countries.

Jeffrey D. Sachs focused on the key issue of whether the debt crisis had emerged primarily because of internal policy errors as per Lal or external shocks as per Simonsen. He acknowledged that policy errors were a factor but doubted seriously that 40 countries had sharply expanded their budget deficits simultaneously. Since about half the debtors had *improved* terms of trade just before the crisis, he concluded that the sharp rise in dollar interest rates had the greatest impact. This effect operated through several channels: a basic change in the ratio of export growth to interest rates paid on outstanding debts, increased capital flight, appreciation of their currencies (which were de facto pegged to the dollar), declines in real investment, and disintermediation of domestic banking systems due to the intensified competition of the dollar.

Juergen B. Donges, to the contrary, suggested that the capital inflow to many LDCs during the 1970s was not used productively. Many developing countries continued to record good performance despite the external shocks. He also felt that the IMF was pursuing adequate supply-side approaches.

John Williamson agreed that the IMF pursued some supply-side policies, but also agreed with Simonsen that better IMF–World Bank coordination was needed. He criticized the rapidity of the adjustment process that had been imposed on Latin America, producing recessions and increasing inflation through excessive devaluations, and the retrenchment in Fund programs under pressure from the United States and a few other major industrial countries from about the middle of 1981.

Gerardo M. Bueno rejected the excessive focus on external shocks that frequently dominated discussion of these issues in the developing countries themselves but noted that the industrial countries had to avoid protectionism to permit Balassa's outward-oriented strategies to succeed. Rapid inflation was costly, and growth must sometimes be sacrificed to curtail it. There were frequent distortions in relative prices: interest rates, wages, exchange rates, and prices of publicly subsidized commodities. His own country (Mexico) had erred in foreseeing perpetually rising oil prices and negative real interest rates.

Manu R. Shroff noted that the avoidance of external imbalances should be viewed as a collective good, pursued by all. However, the Europeans evidently liked the American current account deficit (per Herbert Giersch) and the Japanese seemed to like their surplus (per Masaru Yoshitomi). The LDCs, however, need equilibrium in the industrial world to achieve their own stable recoveries. He suggested that Japan should provide more official aid and that the United States should use its "seigniorage" to increase capital flows to the Third World, and that LDCs that had not borrowed extensively in the past (such as India) should now be benefiting as a result.

Ahn Seung-Chul recounted the recent development path of Korea. He noted that the rapid growth of the 1970s had ultimately produced rapid inflation and an extensive role for government, with negative growth resulting in 1980. Adjustment had been pursued actively, however, through a combination of simple austerity, strong incomes policy (including wage restraint and freezes on government spending and rice prices) and structural adjustment (especially the elimination of industry-specific subsidies). The results were gratifying by 1983–85: growth of 7 percent to 8 percent, inflation under 2 percent, and a current account deficit under 2 percent of GNP. However, the "rewards" for this performance from the industrial countries seem to be increased protection and demands for "graduation," leading him to wonder what lies at the end of the adjustment effort.

William R. Cline praised Simonsen's paper, but defended as necessary and even desirable the temporary "outward transfer of resources" from debtor countries. They needed to continue reducing their debt-export ratios, could achieve economic growth even with such transfers, and had discovered that lower import levels were sustainable in any event. Cline also noted that the debtor countries could change their own exchange rates, and thus need not suffer competitive losses because of the rise in the dollar, although he added that the strong dollar would hurt them in other ways even if they began pegging to a basket of currencies.

Cline also posed two questions for Simonsen: *which* "supply-side" changes would he advocate that the IMF promote, particularly without any increase in its own resources, and what was his best guess concerning the outcome of the debt situation if the banks were to offer Mexico-type rescheduling packages for all major debtors? Cline himself would advocate an IMF compensatory facility for interest-rate increases and action by the banks to provide "reimbursable interest-averaging caps" on their loans to debtor countries.

Rehman Sobhan sharply attacked US policies as they affected the developing countries. He suggested that the industrial countries produced recession and protectionism, rather than any positive rewards, keeping the developing countries on a "treadmill." He called for an LDC political response to the US policy mix and other unhelpful policies in the industrial countries and for "collective resistance" to "unilateral interest-rate increases."

Mihaly Simai pointed to the onset of long-term problems due to the contemporary requirements for adjustment. Small East European countries were caught in a squeeze between the slow structural adjustment of the industrial countries and the rapid competitive growth of the newly industrialized countries (NICs). There were limits to the potential inflow of capital, and he feared that protection in the developed nations was growing and could endure. One result was increased social tension domestically, which made constructive adjustment more difficult. There was great need to construct a framework within which coordinated policy responses could be developed.

José Antonio Ocampo echoed Lal's emphasis on internal transfer problems. Real devaluations required increased domestic transfers, and the amount of necessary refinancing determined the severity of the problem. The inflation tax was ineffective in Latin America.

Replying to the comments of the group, Mario Henrique Simonsen concluded that Brazil could grow by 6 percent annually (instead of the projected 4 percent) except for the pressures of internal inflation. Since 1974, Brazil's GNP had risen by 44 percent; real imports had fallen by 50 percent; and real exports had climbed by 60 percent. The implication was that Brazil had used its external borrowings extremely well.

Concerning the IMF, Simonsen argued that it should promote (even "force") wage-price flexibility and the elimination of most aspects of indexation. Most of its demand-side measures were all right, but its models and theoretical sophistication needed to be improved.

Lal, contrary to Professor Sobhan, thought there had been great success in maintaining open markets for the exports of developing countries. Jamal, on the other hand, endorsed Sobhan's criticisms; he noted that Tanzania, after adjusting to the breakup of the East African Community and the war against Idi Amin, now had to adjust to the IMF, but suffered a 30 percent fall in coffee prices just after concluding a program with the Fund and got only partial and belated compensation from a World Bank structural adjustment loan.

Balassa, in a concluding comment, noted that outward-oriented African countries had experienced a 40 percent increase in their export market shares while inward-oriented countries suffered a loss of 20 percent. Balassa thought the IMF *had* pushed for increased flexibility and exchange rate changes in Africa. Furthermore, he endorsed Cline's view that developing countries could delink their exchange rates from the dollar. Finally, he noted that large increases in government spending in Argentina, Brazil, and Mexico had made them acutely vulnerable to external shocks.

7 Policy Conclusions and Recommendations

The policy panel began with a presentation by Richard N. Cooper. He suggested the existence of a greater confluence of interests than some had suggested in the earlier discussion: the recycling efforts of the 1970s had been beneficial for the world economy, everybody (including the developing countries) wanted to reduce inflation after the second oil shock, no one knew how to achieve that objective without inducing a recession, and no one had accurately predicted the severity of the turndown in 1982—which had brought on the debt crisis, and whose origins were still somewhat unclear.

For the medium-run future, Cooper shared Edmond Malinvaud's "cautious optimism." He found the American economy to be in "very good shape," and was also modestly optimistic about Europe—partly because it seemed to be headed toward a labor shortage in the 1990s. For the short run, Cooper was not so optimistic; the United States should cut its budget deficits, but (per Martin S. Feldstein and Mario Henrique Simonsen) the reduction should not be abrupt, and interest rates would not fall dramatically in any event. Too little attention was being paid to monetary policy; real short-term interest rates had remained at 5 percent during 1982, compared with a normal and appropriate rate of zero during recessions.

With respect to exchange rates, Cooper recalled that the problem had two sides: Japan, Germany, and the United Kingdom had opted for tight fiscal policies and relatively easy monetary policies, compounding the difficulties created by the opposite mix in the United States. He advocated analyzing the current problem in three categories: the global level of demand (which had been deliberately reduced to fight inflation), national policy mixes at any given level of activity, and the international implications (especially for exchange rates) of the different national mixes. Cooper concluded by noting that models recently developed by Jeffrey D. Sachs showed that developing countries would be the primary beneficiaries of better policy coordination within the Organization for Economic Cooperation and Development (OECD).

Saburo Okita viewed the US situation as "unsustainable forever," and hoped that changes in the policy mix would produce a "soft landing." He thought the Europeans seemed to be realizing their problems. There was a need for better international sharing of the response to the less developed country (LDC) debt problem, including greater use of the World Bank and the International Development Association (IDA). Japan clearly had a structural problem which produced its current account surplus, so should expand domestic demand and expand its (public and private) capital flows to developing countries.

Stephen Marris expressed optimism concerning the fundamentals in both the United States and Europe but was afraid that inconsistent and uncoordinated national policies would frustate their positive realization. He noted virtually universal agreement on the need to reduce America's budget deficits, and personally feared market responses to continued deficits which would lead to "a loss of financial control." Capital inflow had been keeping US interest rates down and financing about half the increase in US investment; a reversal of that flow would instead push interest rates up. A "soft landing" was improbable, and only a crisis was likely to produce the needed budgetary action—which then, however, might be excessive. Marris also noted the sharp difference of views about US monetary policy, with some wanting to maintain the present course and others wishing to relax—a disagreement he thought would persist when the dollar began its inevitable decline.

Marris thought the rest of the OECD should have emulated the US strategy of fiscal stimulus and tight money. Their monetary policies will be freed when the dollar declines, and the issue will then be how far they should ease—he would opt for real long rates of zero and negative real short rates to offset the recessionary tendencies that will then emanate from the United States. He saw movement toward the view that Europe should expand fiscally, or at least stop tightening, when the United States began to slow down; there was room for such action because of the tightening to date, and he rejected the models which suggested that the European currencies would weaken in response.

Because the US budget cuts would have to be quite substantial (perhaps 3 percent of GNP), the European budget stimuli would also have to be significant (perhaps 2 percent of their GNPs). Europe was unlikely to move rapidly with such counteraction because the adverse effect of dollar depreciation on their trade balances would come only with a lag. The broader lesson was the need for much better coordination, including fiscal policy and exchange rates (especially to avoid overshooting). He would hope that constructive use could be made of the coming crisis, which he saw as inevitable, particularly to place checks on the excessive capital flows that had permitted both the LDC and American deficits to develop so extensively.

I. G. Patel saw two major imbalances in the present world economy: a sharp retrogression in the development of the poorer countries, which had been going well, and an inadequacy of resources (but *not* excessive conditionality) at both the IMF and the World Bank. He wondered whether the United States could raise its saving rate, noting that LDCs facing an analogous problem of budget deficits and reliance on capital inflows would have to do so. On broader adjustment issues, experience showed that the market alone could not provide the answer to basic problems of the trade-off between unemployment and inflation; all successful development cases had included a role for government intervention. For the LDCs, he would emphasize the efficient deployment of resources rather than a focus on outward-oriented strategies, at least for countries that did not export a very high proportion of their GNP.

The general discussion focused first on the US situation. Herbert Giersch agreed with Cooper that budget cuts would produce only modest declines in American interest rates. Real rates had been negative in the 1970s, so we were now experiencing a reaction above long-term norms (exacerbated by the obsolescence of much capital equipment due to the onset of competition from the NICs and the wage-induced pressures for capital-intensive investment). Such high rates were in fact needed to generate adequate supplies of capital, although incomes policies to check wages were also required. Giersch supported tax cuts for structural reasons (rather than demand stimulus).

Answering Cooper, William H. Branson believed that the US recession was caused largely by the announcement of future budget deficits plus tight monetary policy. Contrary to Cooper and Giersch, Richard G. Lipsey believed that US budget correction plus monetary expansion could bring interest rates down by more than 2 percentage points. Alexander Swoboda regarded the direction and credibility of US fiscal action as more important than the magnitude, and as necessary to achieve a soft landing; the alternative was a sharp fall of the dollar and recession. W. Max Corden also placed heavy emphasis on achieving stable policy courses, suggesting that the debt crisis occurred because of an unexpected shift in macroeconomic policy in the industrial countries; he noted that the United States and United Kingdom were particularly volatile and that Germany and Japan tended to be more consistent, and advocated "soft" announcement effects even to the extent of leaking the news gradually. John Williamson subsequently rejected this latter idea, regarding the dribbling out of policy changes as the worst possible advice.

Pentti J. K. Kouri, contrary to most speakers, approved of the recent US policy mix. He thought it was sustainable, needing only a small shift in world portfolios to provide adequate financing for the external deficits, and was good both for the American economy itself and Europe via improved profitability and the boost to export expansion. (Williamson thought that the size of world portfolios was not the key to dollar sustainability and noted that the strong dollar has implied very high interest rates for Europe as well as export expansion.) The United States should eliminate its budget deficit over time, to stop using foreigners' savings to support its own consumption, but still had time to do so gradually. Niels Thygesen also supported the current US mix, and thought that any sharp dollar decline would be halted by the policy response to its own inflationary consequences.

Peter B. Kenen agreed with Cooper that tight money was the main cause of high US interest rates, with Kouri that much of the US capital inflow was sustainable, and with Branson that there can be sharp financial reactions to fiscal policy announcements. If interest rates and the dollar were to come off sharply in response to an indication of significant budget tightening, in fact, it would therefore be very difficult to ease monetary policy further—particularly as a downward bandwagon effect could easily emerge in the exchange markets. Interest rates might then move back up and generate problems for the real economy. As to policy coordination, Kenen wondered whether intervention has been used effectively. A credible commitment could be the key, underwritten by macroeconomic measures.

Willem H. Buiter stressed that the United States had not yet paid for the decline in its inflation rate caused by dollar appreciation. The Federal Reserve should not rush to tighten money when the dollar begins to decline, and should expand when fiscal policy starts to restrain. Mihaly Simai suggested that high American interest rates caused more problems abroad than at home, and that the US trade deficit reflected an increasingly uncompetitive economy—a view rejected by C. Fred Bergsten.

Turning to Europe, Juergen B. Donges argued that the problems were microeconomic and that macroeconomic policy was not central. Policy coordination was needed only in cases where externalities existed, such as the environment and fisheries, which excluded macroeconomics (including for the European Community, EC, although Thygesen noted the value of coordination for trade liberalization). In fact, policy competition was healthy.

Armin Gutowski shared the long-term views of Herbert Giersch. The price of moderate wage increases in Germany had turned out to include excessive job security and codetermination. A decline of the dollar would have a deflationary effect on Germany, so monetary policy could expand and taxes could be cut. He saw some leeway for macroeconomic management, but thought that leeway was limited and would not promote resolution of the unemployment problem in any event.

Yves Berthelot noted that Japan had done increasingly better than Europe concerning both job creation and industrial investment, which did suggest a measure of Europessimism. To respond, Europe should maintain free trade and move to the second stage of the European Monetary System (EMS), substituting the European currency unit (ECU) for the dollar in intra-European finance.

Luigi Spaventa foresaw only a low probability of a soft landing for the United States. An additional problem deriving from a hard landing would be tensions within the EMS, as the DM rose and deflationary pressures set in. He saw a need for a one-shot cut in wages in Italy, but saw no purpose in inducing unemployment by reducing wages throughout Europe. Jacques Artus added that a 10 percent cut in wages could produce a 20 percent increase in employment, but John Williamson thought the minimum wage was much more important than the average wage in that context.

Masaru Yoshitomi opposed resort to Keynesian policies, especially increases in transfer payments, wherever recessions hit. He thought the overall outcome for 1980-82 had not been so bad, though national contingency plans would be needed if the experience of 1982 alone were repeated.

Massimo Russo argued that EC policy coordination was useful, especially in response to the rise in US interest rates. Europe's wage problem related primarily to its need to reduce unemployment, not its international competitive position. He noted that productivity had risen faster in Europe than in the United States without creating new jobs, and doubted much payoff from new fiscal stimulus.

Ralph C. Bryant suggested that the depth of the recent recession was due partly to the failure of each country to consider the international implications of its own actions, and the significance to it of external developments. Nevertheless, policy coordination was viewed in many quarters as impractical and even undesirable, and he admitted the existence of analytical problems with the concept as well as an absence of political will. He saw a need for more empirical work on the effect of US macroeconomic policy on the rest of the world, as called for by Martin S. Feldstein. Amir H. Jamal noted that the Africans, preferably with the help of the international financial institutions, needed to coordinate their policies including their external borrowing.

To close the discussion, each panelist made several final remarks. I. G. Patel noted a strange paradox regarding views toward the developing countries: there was much convergence among industrial and developing nations on the causes of the current problems and remedies for them, including the need to adjust, but also a seeming withdrawal from international responsibility and a plethora of simplistic advice—"let the markets do it."

Stephen Marris agreed with several commentators on the unlikelihood of a credible program to cut the US budget deficit and achieve a soft landing. Slack growth in the rest of the world would keep capital flowing in, however, and the United States *was* different from other debtor countries—but the deficit numbers were becoming massive. He thought Japan could adapt readily to an economic decline in the rest of the world, and in fact help others respond to their problems. He was less confident about Europe—partly because the needed wage adjustment was difficult to achieve in a stagnant economic environment.

Policy coordination was needed and, to achieve the needed policy perspective, both supply and demand and both short-run and long-run approaches were needed.

Okita saw a need to study recent proposals for increased macroeconomic policy coordination between the United States and Japan. He thought the trading system might turn out to be key: Could we seek a new free trade area? On a global or geographically limited basis? Totally or partially? Countries outside the United States needed to develop contingency plans against a decline in the dollar and the US economy.

Cooper thought Giersch might be right about the persistence of high real interest rates, and noted the decline of capital-labor ratios and the obsolescence of much inherited capital equipment due to the two oil shocks. He again downplayed the impact of budget deficits on long-term interest rates in 1982-83, noting that real short-term interest rates—which should not be influenced by the longer run budget outlook à la Branson—had been higher than real long rates, implying a monetary causation. Cooper also supported Mario Henrique Simonsen's suggestion to look carefully at the tax wedge, and the need for greater policy coordination in view of the "monopoly power" of governments to influence key prices, such as that between tradables and nontradables, as a source of potential market failure.

8 Implications for the Research Agendas

Anne O. Krueger initiated the discussion of research agendas by reporting on six priority areas being pursued at the World Bank. First, a major effort had been launched to quantify all trade barriers, including nontariff barriers, across countries and sectors. The goal was to derive a comprehensive index of protection.

In the less developed country (LDC) debt issue, their analysis is focused on the causes of the sharp increase in difficulty in the early 1980s; the decline in external capital inflows seems to swamp the impact of higher interest rates. In addition, they are studying the trade-offs between bank lending and other types of capital flows, including foreign direct investment.

A third issue is how to increase LDC flexibility in responding to changes in the international economic system. How can capital flows be stabilized? How can macroeconomic management tools be improved? How can factor markets, especially for urban labor, be made to function better?

A related question is how to achieve needed policy reforms, such as trade and financial liberalization. Why is it so difficult? Who are for and against such changes?

A fourth major thrust is research on experience with foreign aid and aid effectiveness.

Finally, what are the linkages between short-run stabilization efforts and long-run growth policies? For example, there is obvious "uneasiness" over the lasting implications of International Monetary Fund (IMF) programs. In some cases, the IMF and the World Bank have offered opposite policy recommendations on a given issue, such as taxation of agricultural exports.

Thierry de Montbrial offered an agenda for future research on international economic issues, stressing the interrelationship of economic and political factors and the need to set priorities. His own focus was on policy coordination and cooperation in an interdependent world. Trade flows were rising rapidly but the global economic system, especially since the breakup of fixed exchange rates in 1971, was "disintegrating." Flexible exchange rates were a substitute for cooperation. Isolationist tendencies needed to be replaced by a new "Bretton Woods spirit." But a political stimulus in these directions was essential, to make research on them appear relevant and thus attractive.

There was a major need for better understanding of the causes and effects of exchange rate changes, and of the entire system of flexible rates. Some deny any possibility of defining equilibrium: "*Is* there a stable equilibrium for the dollar?" There is limited knowledge of the extent of capital flows, let alone their impact. For example, will the United States be a capital importer for at least the next 10 years? Have recent changes in tax policy and the regulatory framework produced a structural change in the direction of capital movements?

Another key issue is the relationship between monetary and trade issues, for example, the impact of overvalued currencies on protectionism. The European Monetary System (EMS) needs more analysis. How does it work? What are its implications for the dollar, for policy coordination within Europe and internationally? What is the record of past efforts at policy cooperation in the Organization for Economic Cooperation and Development (OECD) and other international organizations? Without an international monetary framework like Bretton Woods, how can national policy mixes be effectively coordinated?

Finally, Montbrial cited a number of specific issues that he thought needed further work. Does Europe face a "technology gap"; if so, is it reversible via structural changes of the type advocated by Giersch? What are the positive and negative effects of the current and prospective roles for government in economic management, including with regard to military expenditures? The sharp cutback in research on energy issues, reflecting the current glut, was imprudent; oil was "20 times" as important as any other commodity and there may be long-term cycles that promise more trouble in the future.

William H. Branson began the discussion by expressing confidence in the efficiency of the market for research, and therefore doubts about the need to set research priorities in any systematic way. For example, the National Bureau of Economic Research tried simply to engage outstanding economists and encourage them to pursue their own research interests.

On the debt issue, Branson would focus on four issues: Why did the crisis erupt? Were there ex ante signs? What can be learned from the recent experience? Did the credit markets provide "equilibrium credit rationing"? On macroeconomic policy coordination, he pointed out that the results to date from both practice and formal models were disappointing, suggesting only small benefits; would there be more payoff in coordinating *across* substantive issue areas, such as macroeconomics and trade policy?

Branson also highlighted national trade structures and their implications for national interests, including foreign policy interests. In addition, he suggested more work on the conduct of trade policy in environments of imperfect competition, including "strategic trade policies" (which, however, could easily be misused). Finally, he saw need to consider a number of political economy questions: What were the implications of changes in US hegemony, in the "new multilateral framework" described by Ambassador William E. Brock, and of the "economics of anarchy" à la James Buchanan?

Ahn Seung-Chul focused his discussion on adjustment and trade issues. On adjustment, he would emphasize timing and distribution effects. On trade, he asked whether the traditional theoretical foundation was adequate, in light of the exclusion of technology considerations from the Heckscher–Ohlin model and the contemporary importance of intraindustry specialization.

At the policy level, Ahn thought a number of questions needed more attention. What would be the impact of a new trade "round," including the Brock idea of conducting it through bilateral and "small group" discussions? What were the costs and benefits of protection in specific industries? What were the incentives for newly industrialized countries (NICs) to "graduate," and what would they graduate to? What could be done about the huge Japanese trade imbalances with Korea as well as with the United States and the European Community?

Armin Gutowski began the general discussion by noting that most of the issues cited were being addressed in one or more research centers. The problem was thus mainly one of priorities, although it would be hard to agree on them, and he accepted much of Branson's view that the market for research was highly efficient. A major problem, however, was unavailability of adequate information for researchers and, in particular, the need for more exchanges among researchers including much more extensive translation of publications among the different languages. (Giorgio Basevi later opposed devoting substantial resources to translation.) Gutowski also noted a good deal of overlap in current research efforts, which he thought was alright if the overlaps were undertaken in full knowledge of work going on elsewhere—a process that could be promoted by smaller group meetings to discuss research-in-progress in specific subfields, such as trade or monetary affairs.

Richard Portes advocated decentralization of the research process, including wide dissemination of current results and agendas. On substance, he advocated more empirical work on macroeconomic policy and more emphasis on policy coordination on microeconomic issues (such as social security systems). The longer term outlook for relative prices should be studied, drawing on history and demographics as well as economics. Structural studies, on topics such as deregulation and the flexibility of labor markets, should focus on their economic effects.

Herbert Giersch suggested a need for further research on several issues, for example: What were the links between economics and technology (industrial policy was an inadequate focus)? How can economic growth be explained? Where was the role of government harmful, and how could it be eliminated? The scope for greater utilization of incentives should rank high on the agenda; growth was slow and these issues were more important than macroeconomic policy coordination.

Giersch advocated increased use of the public choice approach to policy problems. For example, what would it imply concerning trade liberalization? He, for one, liked Ambassador Brock's proposals for a "trade liberalization club." Could such a focus be helpful in devising an improved role for international organizations? To help the adjustment to competitive pressures from the NICs, analysis was needed of impediments to deregulation and the potential for regional policies. Shocks should be endogenized in analyses; rational expectations models were too limited.

Yoshindo Takahashi focused on the international monetary system, especially the enormous growth of Japan as a creditor country (to over $200 billion by 1988, greater than the United States at its peak in 1982) and the implications of a multiple reserve currency system. Basevi emphasized the long-term effect of real exchange rate changes on national industrial structures, and endorsed the public choice approach to policy coordination (including via the EMS). Mihaly Simai called for more study of the "regulating forces" of the world economy (the key countries and contemporary structural changes) and an emphasis on institutional developments, and advocated an expansion of parallel and joint research among the various centers.

Eduardo Albertal noted that ECIEL, which comprised 59 research institutions in Latin America, had extensive experience in trying to coordinate research agendas and set priorities over the past 20 years. They tended to focus on regional topics and conduct empirical studies. Priorities were set by surveying the interests and capabilities of the member institutions every three or four years; the results were published and a meeting held, at which projects were negotiated and allocated. An academic committee oversees the process.

ECIEL was currently conducting three major studies: on the flexibility of labor markets in six Latin American countries, on governmental social expenditures in four sectors, and on rural productivity in six nations. New projects would be looking at adjustment, the role of the state as a producer, and conflicts between macroeconomic and agricultural policy.

Emery N. Castle thought the market for research was imperfect because of the high degree of specialization in economics. For example, energy issues should be viewed globally but macroeconomic and microeconomic approaches were hard to link. There were numerous studies of agriculture, but they lacked the needed global focus. International environmental issues were less important than energy and agriculture, but needed more input from economics. He would not push for a highly integrated approach to global research, but saw a clear need for more systematic communication on the issues of concern to him.

Peter B. Kenen noted that, since economists are not good at analyzing why particular policy choices are made, there should be more use of "strategic" and oligopoly theory. However, these approaches are not yet sufficiently realistic regarding decision making, so more collaboration is needed between economists and noneconomists, especially political scientists and historians. Such collaboration could help, for example, in weighing the risks and potential gains that attach to the discriminatory aspects of Ambassador Brock's strategy for trade liberalization. Since contingency planning cannot prudently be left to governments, he urged nongovernmental research institutions to take the initiative and to make their work available, publicly or otherwise, to official bodies.

With regard to macroeconomic policy coordination, Kenen thought the precondition was agreement on the functioning of the world economy; there was simply no accepted paradigm at present. Economists need to find a common ground, as a basis for setting priorities and making forecasts. Tony Killick added that the "Third World" concept was not useful, and that a new typology of countries was now needed.

Karl Heinrich Oppenlander disagreed with Ahn, suggesting that trade theory was in fact adequate to address current issues; his own focus would be on a wide range of data problems (including the need for new data, as indicated by the huge "statistical discrepancy" in the global balance of payments data) and on synthesizing the existing "Year 2000" studies. Manu R. Shroff emphasized the need for policy research, focused on setting national priorities toward international issues and formulating positions toward the rest of the world. Rehman Sobhan suggested a retrospective analysis of the impact of past research results, to see what work had been effectively used, as a guide for the future. Gerardo M. Bueno advocated the publication of joint views on policy topics.[1]

José Antonio Ocampo emphasized the need for more research on "massive and violent" economic shocks and adjustment to them. He noted that most models contemplated only modest and linear disturbances, whereas the adjustments required in the real world had sizable distributional and other effects that raised doubts about whether they could be implemented without major social disruption. An example was devaluations exceeding 100 percent, which in turn raised questions about the feasibility of certain exchange rate mechanisms. Another broad area needing more work was second-best policies, such as trade and exchange controls, which were largely ignored in the industrial countries but widely used in developing nations.

---

[1] Citing as an example, *Promoting World Recovery: A Statement on Global Economic Strategy* by Twenty-six Economists from Fourteen Countries (Washington: Institute for International Economics, December 1982).

Appendices

Participants in the Conference
Institute for International Economics,
Washington, September 21–23, 1984

C. Michael Aho
Council on Foreign Relations
New York, NY

Eduardo Albertal
Estudos Conjuntos sobre Integración Econômica Latinoamericana
Rio de Janeiro

Ronald Aqua
United States–Japan Foundation
New York, NY

Jacques Artus
International Monetary Fund
Washington

Bela Balassa
The World Bank
Washington

Giorgio Basevi
Universita degli Studi di Bologna
Italy

Tom Bayard
Ford Foundation
New York, NY

C. Fred Bergsten
Institute for International Economics

Yves Berthelot
Centre d'Etudes Prospectives et d'Informations Internationales
Paris

Jagdish N. Bhagwati
Columbia University
New York, NY

Rodrigo Botero
Servicios de Información
Bogotá

William H. Branson
National Bureau of Economic Research
Cambridge, Mass.

William E. Brock
US Trade Representative
Washington

Ralph C. Bryant
The Brookings Institution
Washington

Gerardo M. Bueno
El Colegio de Mexico

Willem H. Buiter
London School of Economics

Ricardo Carrillo Arronte
Centro de Investigación y Docencia Económicas
Mexico

Emery N. Castle
Resources for the Future
Washington

Richard N. Cooper
Harvard University
Cambridge, Mass.

Hugh Corbet
Trade Policy Research Centre
London

W. Max Corden
The Australian National University
Canberra, Australia

Francis Cripps
University of Cambridge
Cambridge, England

John M. Curtis
Institute for Research on Public Policy
Ottawa

André de Lattre
Institute of International Finance
Washington

Thierry de Montbrial
Institut Français des Relations Internationales
Paris

A. R. Dobell
Institute for Research on Public Policy
Ottawa

Juergen B. Donges
Institut für Weltwirtschaft
Kiel, Federal Republic of Germany

Geza Feketekuty
Office of the US Trade Representative
Washington

Martin S. Feldstein
National Bureau of Economic Research
Cambridge, Mass.

Roberto Fendt, Jr.
Fundação Central de Estudos do Comércio Exterior
Rio de Janeiro

Isaiah Frank
Johns Hopkins University
Washington

Jacob A. Frenkel
University of Chicago
Chicago, Ill.

Herbert Giersch
Institut für Weltwirtschaft
Kiel, Federal Republic of Germany

Armin Gutowski
HWWA-Institut für Wirtschaftsforschung-Hamburg

David Henderson
Organization for Economic Cooperation and Development
Paris

William C. Hood
International Monetary Fund
Washington

Gregory K. Ingram
The World Bank
Washington

Alexis Jacquemin
Centre for European Policy Studies
Brussels

Amir H. Jamal
Minister of State
Tanzania

Louka T. Katseli
Centre of Planning and Economic Research
Athens

Peter B. Kenen
Princeton University
Princeton, NJ

Tony Killick
Overseas Development Institute
London

Mahn Je Kim
Minister of Finance
Republic of Korea

Pentti J. K. Kouri
New York University
New York, NY

Lawrence B. Krause
The Brookings Institution
Washington

Anne O. Krueger
The World Bank
Washington

Deepak Lal
The World Bank
Washington

Roger Lawrence
UN Conference on Trade and Development
Geneva

Richard G. Lipsey
C. D. Howe Institute
Toronto

Frank E. Loy
German Marshall Fund of the United States
Washington

Peter Ludlow
Centre for European Policy Studies
Brussels

Samir A. Makdisi
American University of Beirut

Edmond Malinvaud
Institut National de la Statistique et des Etudes Economiques
Paris

Manea Manescu
State Council of the Socialist Republic of Romania

Stephen Marris
Institute for International Economics

Paul W. McCracken
American Enterprise Institute
The University of Michigan
Ann Arbor, Mich.

Michael Michaely
Maurice Falk Institute for Economic Research in Israel
Jerusalem

Joseph S. Nye, Jr.
Harvard University
Cambridge, Mass.

José Antonio Ocampo
FEDESARROLLO
Bogotá

Saburo Okita
Institute for Domestic and International
Policy Studies
Tokyo

Osman Okyar
Foreign Policy Institute
Ankara

Karl Heinrich Oppenlander
IFO-Institut für Wirtschaftsforschung-Munich

François-Xavier Ortoli
Commission of the European Communities
Brussels

I. G. Patel
London School of Economics

Joan Pearce
Royal Institute of International Affairs
London

Torsten Persson
Institute for International Economic Studies
Stockholm

James Piereson
John M. Olin Foundation
New York, NY

Richard Portes
Centre for Economic Policy Research
London

Massimo Russo
Commission of the European Communities
Brussels

Jeffrey D. Sachs
Harvard University
Cambridge, Mass.

Ahn Seung-Chul
Korea Development Institute
Seoul

John W. Sewell
Overseas Development Council
Washington

Manu R. Shroff
Indian Council for Research on International Economic Relations
New Delhi

Ammar Siamwalla
Thailand Development Research Institute
Bangkok

Mihaly Simai
Hungarian Academy of Sciences
Budapest

Mario Henrique Simonsen
Getulio Vargas Foundation
Rio de Janeiro

Rehman Sobhan
Bangladesh Institute of Development Studies
Dacca

Luigi Spaventa
Instituto di Economia
University of Rome

Alexander Swoboda
Graduate Institute of International Studies
Geneva

Yoshindo Takahashi
Nomura Research Institute
London

Tsutomu Tanaka
Economic Research Institute
Tokyo

Niels Thygesen
Centre for European Policy Studies
Brussels

Otto Vogel
Institut der deutschen Wirtschaft
Cologne, Federal Republic of Germany

Rimmer de Vries
Morgan Guaranty Trust Company
New York, NY

Kiichi Watanabe
Japan Center for International Finance
Tokyo

Marina v.N. Whitman
General Motors Corporation
New York, NY

John Williamson
Institute for International Economics
Washington

Masaru Yoshitomi
Economic Planning Agency
Tokyo

APPENDIX B Glossary and Acronyms of Research Institutions Contributing to Appendix C

BR	The Brookings Institution, Washington
CCEPS	Claremont Center for Economic Policy Studies, California
CEPII	Centre d'Etudes Prospectives et d'Informations Internationales, Paris
CEPR	Centre for Economic Policy Research, London
CEPS	Centre for European Policy Studies, Brussels
CIDE	Centro de Investigación y Docencia Económicas, Mexico
CIEPLAN	Corporación de Investigaciones Económicas para Latinoamerica, Chile
DAE	Department of Applied Economics, University of Cambridge
EC	European Community, Brussels
ECIEL	Estudios Conjuntos sobre Integración Econômica Latinoamericana, Rio de Janeiro
EPA	Economic Planning Agency, Tokyo
FPI	Foreign Policy Institute, Ankara
HWWA	HWWA-Institut für Wirtschaftsforschung-Hamburg
IER	Instituto di Economia, University of Rome
IFO	IFO-Institut für Wirtschaftsforschung-Munich
IIE	Institute for International Economics, Washington
IIES	Institute for International Economic Studies, Stockholm

103

INSEE   Institut National de la Statistique et des Etudes Economiques, Paris

IPA   Institute for Policy Analysis, University of Toronto

IRPP   The Institute for Research on Public Policy, Ottawa

JCIF   Japan Center for International Finance, Tokyo

KDI   Korea Development Institute, Seoul

KEPE   Centre of Planning and Economic Research, Athens

KIEL   Kiel Institut für Weltwirtschaft, West Germany

NBER   National Bureau of Economic Research, Inc., Cambridge, Massa-
                 chusetts

NRI   Nomura Research Institute, Tokyo and London

ODC   Overseas Development Council, Washington

ODI   Overseas Development Institute, London

RFF*   Resources for the Future, Washington

RI   Royal Institute of International Affairs, London

---

* The work at Resources for the Future deals mainly with commodity and energy issues and is not included with the general subject areas covered in appendix C.

APPENDIX C Summary of Research Agendas Submitted by Participating Institutions

The following is an outline of work in progress as submitted by some participants in the Institute's conference on "Imbalances in the World Economy," Washington, DC, September 21–23, 1984. The acronyms used to identify institutions carrying out the individual projects are defined in appendix B.

Global Issues

TRADE

Rethinking the International Trading Regime (BR)   Evaluates the current international trading regime with an emphasis on its present problems and future prospects. Will give special attention to topics covering the role of LDCs in the General Agreement on Tariffs and Trade (GATT) and issues for future GATT negotiating rounds.

World Industrial Prospects (CEPII)   Addresses competitiveness of industrial sectors, considering markets as well as costs and technology, emphasizing the relationships among Japan, the United States, and the European Community (EC). Studies volume and value of exports and market shares and estimates elasticities of substitution.

International Trade (CEPR)   Studies structural change and shifts in comparative advantage, imperfect competition, industrial policy, customs unions in theory and practice, internal and external trade patterns in the EC.

European-US Trade Relations (CEPS)   Analyzes and quantifies the major current areas of European criticism of US policies and US criticism of European policies: agriculture, industry, trade in services and high technology industries, embargoes and trade policies, differences in institutional settings, and interaction between macroeconomic developments, trade, and investment.

Common Commercial Policy (RI)   Analyzes the role of EC member states and of the Commission in molding a common EC commercial policy; investigates how the policy is pursued in international negotiations in GATT, the Organization for Economic Cooperation and Development (OECD), the United Nations Conference on Trade and Development (UNCTAD), and other organizations. Asks to what extent the Commission is constrained by the mandate agreed in advance of negotiations, and what opportunities exist for member states to influence the Community's stance while negotiations are in progress. Pays particular attention to the next round of GATT negotiations and the British interest in liberalization of trade in services, which will be on the agenda for the first time.

Europe in the World Economy (CEPS)   Analyzes European policy options in light of the major structural changes in industry and the global economy, developments in high technology and services, the growth of intra-industry agreements, and changes in financial markets.

Macroeconomic Impact of Commercial Openness and International Financial Movements (CIEPLAN)   Estimates export and import equations, both at aggregated and disaggregated levels. Focuses on topics central to the debate on macroeconomic adjustment in Latin America in the 1980s.

The Future of the Multilateral Trade and Financial System (IRPP)

Adjustment to Trade-created Dislocations (IIE)   Draws on past US and non-US experience to assess the impact on labor markets and industry of adjustment requirements triggered by dislocations of all types, and assesses the record of past policy responses in an effort to devise new approaches to positive trade adjustment.

The Next International Trade Negotiations (IIE)   Analyzes the issues which should and could be addressed in "the next MTN," and how they could be approached by the major trading nations.

International Trade Topics (IIES)   Empirical studies of problems in international trade, especially comparative advantage and factor mobility.

Comparative Project on International Structures and Foreign Trade of Major Industrial Countries (France, Germany, Italy, United Kingdom, United States) (INSEE)   Uses data from 1975–82 for 135 industries.

The Significance of the Generalized System of Preferences (GSP) and Its Links with Other Community Aid Policies (HWWA)   Addresses the 1984 GSP revision and its redevelopment for 1985–90.

Patterns and Directions of Trade Flows (IPA)   Uses new economic models to explain patterns and directions of trade, concentrating on the imperfectly competitive nature of most markets and firms' reactions to changes in trade conditions.

The Changing Structure of World Production and Trade: Implications for the United States (NBER)   Explores causes and effects of differential growth in productivity and competitiveness, growth of manufacturing in developing countries, competition among the United States, Europe, and Japan in developing countries.

American Trade Relations (NBER)   Analyzes the causes and effects of recent and prospective US trade policy initiatives, with detailed examination of effects of specific trade policy instruments such as DISC and countervailing duties.

Strategic Behavior and Trade Policy (NBER)   Analyzes trade policy in a world of imperfect competition and strategic behavior.

Trade and Industrial Policy (ODC)   Proposes measures to strengthen the international trading system, particularly as it affects the developing countries.

Europe and Protection: The Current Debate (RI)   Considers the debate about protection in European trade and industrial policy, deals with recent trade measures and French proposals on Community industrial policy, and analyzes the attitudes of several member states toward them. Discusses the classical argument for free trade, the case for protection in the presence of scale economies, and the case of R&D-intensive sectors, and relates them to various sectors of European industry. Also deals with exchange rate policy and protection.

Financing Export Credit: The Economics of Guarantees and Subsidies (RI)   Assesses what proportion of officially guaranteed export credits the market would not take on and evaluates the subsidy implicit in government guarantees for such credits, applying the theory of credit rationing and borrowing with default risk. Investigates the relationship between interest-rate differentials for different currencies and exchange rate changes, using recent work on the relation between exchange rates and interest rates, and examines the subsidies implicit in a system of uniform minimum interest rates for all currencies and the basis for an alternative system of differentiated minimum rates.

FINANCE/MACROECONOMICS

The International Monetary System (BR)   Concentrates on exchange rate variability and exchange market intervention, intergovernmental consultations about macroeconomic issues, East-West financial relations, and the US vision of the International Monetary Fund (IMF) and other international institutions.

Exchange Rate Behavior and International Effects on the US Macroeconomy (CCEPS)   Analyzes the effects of currency substitution and international capital flows on US monetary conditions, risk premiums and the term structure of interest-rate differentials and forward rates, and the influence of limited time horizons and supplies of funds in the foreign exchange market on exchange rate responses to budget deficits and other disturbances.

International and Domestic Influences on National Monetary Policies (CCEPS)   Analyzes possible inflationary biases in the operations of democratic processes and the effects of alternative domestic and international monetary regimes; includes developing countries.

The Dominant Economies (CEPII)   Centers on the United States, Japan, Germany, France and the United Kingdom, involving comparative analysis and emphasizing the effects of external shocks. Focuses on productivity growth, employment, and terms of trade of manufacturing products, and the impact on inflation.

Global Balance of Payments Patterns (CEPII)   Traces the global financial tensions resulting from shifts in energy costs and debt service flows, including the effects on exchange rates of major currencies. Based on a globally reconciled balance of payments CEPII data base.

International Macroeconomics (CEPR)   Focuses on economic interdependence and macroeconomic policy coordination, policy design in an open economy, and causes and consequences of exchange rate misalignments. Also looks at recent economic history in the open economy context.

Compact Model (EC)   Presents an econometric model of the EC aggregate economy linked to well-known models of the United States (FED-MCM) and Japan (EPA), and rest-of-the-world equations for raw materials, trade, and debt.

Research on Strategic Problems of the World Economy (DAE)   Develops an analytical and empirical framework for evolution of strategic problems facing Western Europe within the world economy as a whole. Does a quantitative simulation of the model emphasizing interrelationships between growth of real demand, flows of trade, relative prices, and financial deficits or surpluses of different regions.

Trilateral Monetary and Exchange Rate Management: The Interest of Germany

(HWWA)   Starting from McKinnon's and Williamson's proposals, presents pros and cons of nonsterilized intervention from a German perspective.

Structural Change and Macroeconomic Policy (KEPE)   Links the process of development and the emergence of rigidities that make stabilization policy in open economies increasingly ineffective.

Problems of Structural Change and Long-term Growth in Major Industrial Countries (KIEL)

International Monetary and Financial Situation (CIDE)   Analyzes current monetary and financial events and their impact on real and monetary variables.

Unemployment, Relative Factor Prices, and Capital-Labor Substitution (EC)   Models production functions for Germany, France, Italy, the United Kingdom, and the United States to distinguish between "classical" and "Keynesian" unemployment.

EPA World Econometric Model (EPA)   Presents a quarterly model composed of nine Keynesian individual country models (summit seven, Australia, and Korea) and an international trade linkage submodel, to quantify the effects of fiscal and monetary shocks under fixed and flexible rates.

Floating Exchange Rates and International Specialization (IER)   Does a theoretical and empirical analysis of the consequences that long-lasting movements of exchange rates, resulting in a persistent real appreciation of the currency concerned, may have on the sectoral composition of output. Hypothesizes that such consequences are not symmetric with those of a real depreciation and that they are irreversible, thereby affecting international specialization.

The Exchange Rate with Persistently Lax Fiscal Policy and Tight Monetary Policy (IER)   Considers a small open economy in which, while the public-sector borrowing requirements are such as to cause a rapid growth of the debt-GDP ratio, authorities aim at a monetary base target; refers to Italian case.

Misalignment of Exchange Rates (IFO)   Looks at causes and effects of exchange rates on international trade, growth, and employment in an empirical study focusing on the problems of open European economies.

International Macroeconomics (IIES)   Focuses on the importance for macroeconomic development of wage formation and exchange rates, relative prices, and price of intermediate inputs. Examines payment and current account balances and their effects on savings and investment.

The Multiple Reserve Currency System (IIE)   Analyzes the impact of multiple reserve evolution on exchange rates and the stability of the international monetary system.

Deficits and the Dollar: The World Economy at Risk (IIE)   Examines the impact of the overvalued dollar on the US and world economies, with policy recommendations both for promoting a "soft landing" and coping with any precipitate depreciation that may occur.

Second-Best Responses to Currency Imbalances (IIE)   Explores the panoply of second-best, direct manipulations of capital and current account transactions that have been used on occasion to cope with currency disequilibria and how they might fare under contemporary conditions.

The Exchange Rates of Factors Influencing the Development of the Real Exchange Rate (HWWA)   A time-series analysis of medium- and long-run movements of exchange rates of United States, Japan, and major EC members.

International Monetary Arrangements (HWWA)   Analyzes the economic and political conditions for a well-functioning international monetary system on the basis of historical experience.

Macroeconomic Policy Coordination among Industrial Countries (INSEE)

International Differences in Economic Behavior (INSEE)   Models small countries with quantity rationing.

International Financial and Foreign Exchange Markets (JCIF)   Examines joint intervention in foreign exchange markets, Euromarkets, and their influence on domestic markets, and arbitrage among financial markets, in theoretical studies.

The Nature and the Outlook for National Business Cycles and their International Intersection (KIEL)   Uses econometric methods for economic policy simulation. Other projects study fundamental aspects of the money supply, inflation, and exchange rates.

The Real-Financial Nexus (NBER)   Studies the interaction between exchange rates and "real" variables; analyzes financial markets as international transmitters of real disturbances.

Exchange Rate Determination (NBER)   Analyzes determinants of exchange rate fluctuations; studies efficiency of foreign exchange markets and variability of risk premiums.

International Monetary Coordination (NBER)   Studies potential gains from international coordination of macroeconomic policies, strategic behavior between governments and private agents, and design of rules permitting cooperative outcomes.

Multiple Currency System: The History and Possible Future Role of the Yen (NRI)

International Finance (ODC)   Explores development-oriented aspects of international finance, particularly whether the volume of total resource transfers is adequate to adjust to changes in the world economy.

IFO Forecasting Exercise (IFO)   Analyzes world trade and cyclical impacts resulting from other industrial countries.

Short-term Macroeconomic Performance of the US, Japanese, and European Economies (IFO)   Presents periodic observation and assessment of the US, Japanese, and European economies.

FINANCIAL MARKETS AND INVESTMENT

Issues in International Banking: A Canadian Perspective (IRPP)

Internationalization of Japanese Financial Markets (JCIF)   Examines the Tokyo capital market, recent developments and future perspectives; government bond management policy; fiduciary powers in banking systems of other countries and problems of the Tokyo market; and internationalization of Japanese enterprises.

Internationalization of the Yen and the Changing Pattern in the Flow of Capital (NRI)

Financial Deregulation in Advanced Countries and Effects on Monetary Policy (NRI)

Financing of Investment (EC)   Studies EC facilities for investment financing and compares them with those of the United States and Japan.

New International Arrangements for Foreign Direct Investment (IIE)   Analyzes current impediments to direct investment and the possible utility of new international arrangements to improve the outlook.

Outward Investment (RI)   Examines the investment climate, both economic and regulatory, in the principal host countries. Also discusses whether changes are required in British policy in the context of domestic economic objectives, relations with host countries, and international efforts to establish codes of conduct.

NORTH-SOUTH

North-South Models (CEPR)   Studies trade and industrial structure in the 1980s and the political economy of protectionism.

Euro-South Relations (CEPS)   Focuses on EC food strategy and trade in agricultural commodities; will expand to cover broader problems of trade and finance.

Structural Transformations in Advanced Economies and Their Impact on Semi-industrialized Countries (CIDE)   Analyzes the restructuring of industry and redeployment in developed countries and effects on semi-industrialized countries. Focuses on automotive and "off-shore" industries.

EC and the Third World: An Annual Survey (ODI)

Trade and Financing Strategies for the NICs (ODI)   Presents multicountry and detailed case studies of Colombia, Egypt, Malaysia, Peru, and Thailand. Examines the record of NICs in the 1970s, and analyzes alternative strategies.

Import Needs and Potential of Third World Countries (ODI)   Analyzes past and future trends of LDC imports and explores medium- and long-run LDC import needs.

DEVELOPMENT

Technological Advance and Economic Development (EC)   Studies the entry of technical innovations into the capital stock and the skills of the labor force, initially using the EC industry data bank.

The Impact of Foreign Aid on World Economic Growth (EPA)   Quantifies the impact of foreign aid on economic growth of developing and developed countries.

Economics of Developing Countries (IIES)   Emphasizes the links between developed and underdeveloped countries, in predominantly empirical studies relating to direct investment, state enterprises and developing countries, protectionism and trade in industrial goods, and so forth.

Effects of "Own Efforts" on the Development Process (HWWA)   Presents case studies examining efforts of the developing countries and their socioeconomic consequences.

Economic Development of Developing Countries (JCIF)   Examines economic development, especially from the viewpoint of combined savings and investment in theoretical and case studies. Looks at the role of international organizations and the relationship between exports and debt.

Economic Development and International Integration of Developing Countries (KIEL) Focuses on trade strategies for industrialization, agricultural development, and export diversification.

Liberalization in Developing Countries (NBER) Analyzes the sequence of liberalization in developing countries between trade and finance, the effects on world markets, and feedback to the US economy.

Development Assistance Reconsidered (ODI) Analyzes the underlying theoretical and ethical positions of the chief critics of aid.

Development Strategies and Development Assistance (ODC) Identifies development strategies that work effectively toward poverty alleviation and analyzes the levels and amounts of foreign assistance.

THE DEBT PROBLEM

External Debt Problem in Latin America (CIEPLAN) Analyzes factors determining the debt crisis and their interrelation with national economic policies. Includes a comparative analysis of mechanisms regulating capital movements in the different countries.

Debt Issues (CIEPLAN) Studies evolution of external debt crisis in Latin America (1982–84) and effects of IMF agreements on domestic economies.

The Debt Capacity of Developing Countries (HWWA) Sets out conditions for the success of growth processes financed by foreign credits.

Financial Intermediation Beyond the Debt Crisis (IIE) Explores possible new means for channeling private and official capital to the debtor nations to finance their ongoing balance of payments needs.

Country Risks and the World Debt Problem (JCIF) Includes a general discussion and country studies of the world debt problem, ideas on the solution of the debt problem, the influence of the debt problem on banks, and individual studies on 17 major developing countries.

Korea's Debt Management and Policy Options (KDI)

Debt and International Financial Markets (NBER) Examines the causes and consequences of the developing-country debt problem, implications of alternative scenarios on the stability of financial markets, and effects on the US economy.

EAST-WEST

Energy, Economics, and Foreign Policy in the Soviet Union (BR) Analyzes Soviet developments in energy production, consumption, and trade for the next decade and assesses implications for the world economy, East-West economic relations, and Soviet foreign policy.

Economic Reform in the Soviet Union (BR) Analyzes recent problems in Soviet economic performance, prospects and options for economic reform, and the implications for Soviet relations with the West and Eastern Europe.

The Socialist Economies (CEPII) Studies the economies of the Soviet Union, China, and Eastern Europe, with particular attention to the international economic implications of developments in Socialist countries.

Compensatory Transactions and International Trade (KEPE)   Explores possibilities of trade expansion between Greece and East European countries.

International Organizations and Socialist Countries: Possibilities for an Intensification of Trade Relations, Cooperation, and Financial Relations Between East and West (HWWA)   Studies East-West cooperation through international organizations such as the GATT and the IMF.

Economic and Scientific-Technical Cooperation Between East and West in Third Countries, Particularly in Developing Countries (HWWA)

Regional and Sectoral Issues

TRADE AND FINANCE

The Future Course of Canadian-US Economic Relations (BR)   Discusses key issues in US-Canadian economic relations, particularly investment regulations, trade legislation, energy policies, and environment issues.

The Role of US Investment in US-Mexican Economic Relations (BR)   Studies the nature and effects of US investment in Mexico, policies and perceptions relating to such investment, and its impact on employment and the balance of payments in both countries.

The EMS in the International Monetary System (CEPS)   Studies the European currency unit-dollar relationship, exchange rates and monetary policies in the European Monetary System (EMS), German monetary policy and policy options in the face of a fluctuating dollar and EMS exchange rate commitments, the process of surveillance and policy coordination in Europe, and the participation of sterling in the EMS. Develops a systematic study of hard currencies in the EMS, and lays the foundation for a subproject on the economic, institutional, and political preconditions of "phase 2" of the EMS.

The Role of the ECU (RI)   Examines the advantages of and necessary measures for extending the role of the ECU. Considers expressed reservations and strategies for dealing with them and for negotiating an agreement among EC governments.

Monetary Unions and the European Monetary System (INSEE)   Focuses on the coordination of monetary policies within the system.

European Macroeconomic Policy and Prospects (CEPS)   Reports annually on macroeconomic policies and prospects for the European Community and presents detailed papers on specific issues including, for example, US deficits, the dollar, and Europe.

Industrial Policy in Europe (RI)   Surveys the advantages and disadvantages for European companies of cooperating with other European companies as against non-European companies, notably from the United States and Japan. Assesses obstacles to cooperation between European companies, including internal trade barriers, public procurement policies, and some aspects of competition policy, as well as differences in industrial structure (particularly regarding cooperation between nationalized and private companies), in domestic industrial policy (aids, R&D), and in the extent of government intervention in the economy.

The Determinants of Interregional Factor Flows, Allocation of Resources, and

Specialization in the European Community (KIEL)   Analyzes the conditions for European revitalization, in particular, common agricultural policies and trade policies for manufactures.

The Middle East, Turkey, and the Atlantic Alliance (FPI)   Covers the strategic, political, and economic role of Turkey in the region.

Pacific Cooperation for Trade Negotiations (KDI)   Recommends Pacific Basin country cooperation to achieve global trade negotiations that would improve their market access.

Prospects for the Pacific Basin (NRI)   Identifies trends in industrial structure adjustments and developing trade patterns.

Prospects for African Primary Agricultural Commodity Exports and the Scope for EC Intervention (ODI)   Assesses both past performance and future prospects of a set of specific commodities/countries; identifies possible EC assistance interventions.

Labor Conditions, Wages, and Export-led Industrialization in Asian Countries (ODI)   Establishes changes that are attributable to the export-led strategy, based on selected studies in Korea, Malaysia, Taiwan, and Thailand.

Economic Policies, Employment, and Income Distribution in Latin America (ECIEL)   Analyzes the impact of recent economic policies on labor markets and employment, wage levels, and income distribution in the context of different kinds of stabilization programs.

SECTORAL STUDIES

Preparing for the Next Oil Shock (BR)   Examines the international dimension of preparing for the next oil shock. Discusses possibilities for coordinated action among industrial countries to mitigate the impact of supply interruption, and stock management policies and coordinated import fees.

Targeting Technology: International Competition and National Intervention in Computer Development (BR)   Presents a comparative economic history of international competition in computers, controlling the international flow of technology, and the industrial organization of US research, and considers international trade rules governing national support for technology.

Internal and External Constraints Affecting the Largest Industrial Companies in Europe (CEPS)   Builds a data base on the performance of the largest European companies; monitors concurrent parallel work in the United States.

A European Future in High Technology (CEPS)   Looks at innovation in international perspective, industrial structure and innovation, and public policy and innovation. Specific issues include large firm innovation strategies in Western Europe, labor markets, education and industrial structure, capital markets and industrial structure, and the role of public procurement.

International Trade Competition and Cooperation in the High Technology Sector (HWWA)   Discusses possible national and international approaches to trade and industrial policies in the high technology sector from a European perspective.

Sectoral and Bilateral Approaches to International Trade Problems: The Case of the Automobile Industry (HWWA)   Analyzes trends in international production and distribution of automobiles and national responses.

Agricultural Protectionism in Industrial Countries (IFO)

Trade Controls in Three Industries: The Automobile, Steel, and Textiles Cases (IIE)   Analyzes the distributional and international effects of existing and proposed restrictions in the three largest manufacturing sectors currently experiencing trade protection.

Country-Specific Studies

TRADE

Trade in Services (KEPE)   Examines Greek tourism, shipping, insurance, and other services.

An Econometric Analysis of Export Performance (KEPE)   Presents an econometric analysis of factors determining disaggregated export performance for Greece.

Structural Problems of the Balance of Payments and their Effects on the Structure of the Greek Economy (KEPE)

Competitiveness of the Tourist Sector in Greece (KEPE)

A Study of Price Formation and Stabilization (CIEPLAN)   Examines the price mechanism of the tradable sector with special emphasis on the "law of one price," in theoretical and econometrical studies.

Economic Prospects of Newly Emerging Trade Partners and Analysis of Implications for Trade with Canada: The ASEAN Group (IRPP)

Nontariff Barriers and Effective Protection in Canadian Industries (IRPP)

Canadian Trade Policy in a Changing World (IRPP)

Turkey's Relationship with Europe (FPI)

The Current Structure of German Trade (HWWA)   Updates an earlier study using the recent experience with a "weak" D-mark.

Causes and Factors of the International Competitive Position of German Industry (IFO)   Contributes to the analysis of structural change in Germany.

The Importance of the Production, Exports, and Reserves of Gold, Platinum, and Diamonds for the "Room for Maneuver" in Soviet Trade Policy (HWWA)

International Trade Policy Issues from a Korean Perspective (KDI)   Surveys major international trade policy issues from a Korean perspective and recommends government positions in international negotiations.

Korea's Export Patterns in a Long-term Perspective (KDI)   Identifies the roles of dynamic comparative advantage factors in shifting the Korean export structure.

Liberalization of Services Trade and Policy Proposals for Japan (NRI)

Trade Friction and Japan's Export-Import Structure (NRI)

Structural Policies for Traditional and Declining Sectors in Japan (IFO)

FINANCE/MACROECONOMICS

OPEC's Financial Power (BR)   Examines the impact of financial decisions of the OPEC nations on the international system—including the role of OPEC surpluses in the international system, developing countries, and international institutions (the IMF and the World Bank) and ways the West is affected by and can affect OPEC investments.

Resource Reallocation in France (BR) Explores the evolution of France's economic structure since World War II, specifically considering French economic growth, indicative planning, as well as French industrial policy and its implications for US industrial policy.

The Australian Economy: A View from the North (BR) Examines the performance and problems of the Australian economy, concentrating on issues including social welfare, natural resources, comparative advantage, and the financial system.

The Japanese Economy and Relations with the United States (BR) Traces the evolution of the Japanese economy since 1973 and evaluates the consequences of the end of the technology catch-up and other structural factors including their impact on Japan's balance of payments. Analyzes economic relations with the United States in light of these developments.

Domestic Financial Systems (CIEPLAN) Studies Chilean financial market liberalization, the impact of international capital movements, and their effects on savings and investment.

Crawling Peg vs. Discrete Adjustment of Exchange Rates: Suggested Evidence from Greece (KEPE) Presents an econometric analysis of real exchange rate behavior under the two regimes.

Study on Japan's Savings (EPA) Attempts to explain the puzzle of continued high saving by Japanese households. Discusses macroeconomic factors (including the life cycle theory of savings) unique to Japan and the taxation system.

The Effects of External Economic Forces in Canada (IPA) Explores the extent to which Canadian interdependence with the rest of the world limits independent domestic macroeconomic policies.

Britain's Changing Role in the Provision of Financial Services (RI) Examines the implications of rapid changes in the UK financial services sector in the context of international competitiveness and considers international regulatory issues.

Japan in the International Financial System (RI) Examines past changes and considers potential developments; analyzes the probable effects on Japan's economy, on international capital markets, on the position of foreign financial institutions in Japan and Japanese institutions overseas, and on the role of the yen as a trading, investment, and reserve currency.

Other Issues

Public Choice Analysis of International Economic Relations (CCEPS) Applies public choice analysis to various aspects of the political economy of international economic relations including evaluation of the adequacy and possible scope for improvements in international monetary relations, analysis of international and domestic macroeconomic influences on protectionism in the United States, analysis of the various roles for economic sanctions and the factors that influence their effectiveness, institutional aspects of the trade and industrial policy debate, US immigration policy, and allocation of US development assistance funds.

Economic Policy and National Accounting in Inflationary Conditions (EC)   Provides a conceptual framework and comprehensive data set for sectoral financial balances adjusted for the impact of inflation (Germany, France, Italy, the United Kingdom, and Belgium); includes a related study on crowding out.

Operations and Decisions of International Firms (IPA)   Explores forces affecting multinational corporations' decisions to invest, produce, and locate production. Includes growth-induced changes in supply and demand conditions; effects of changes in the international division of labor; effects of trade patterns, implication of tariffs and subsidies, and the role of the state as a regulator.

Comparison of US and UK Dominance of the World Economy (IN-SEE)   Compares the dominance of the United Kingdom (1860–1930) and the United States (since 1945).

Foreign Policy (ODC)   Contributes to a coherent foreign policy strategy and addresses the relationship between economic and security issues and between regional and global policies.

Other Publications from the Institute

POLICY ANALYSES IN INTERNATIONAL ECONOMICS SERIES

BOOKS

SPECIAL REPORTS

1 **Promoting World Recovery: A Statement on Global Economic Strategy** *by Twenty-six Economists from Fourteen Countries*/December 1982

2 **Prospects for Adjustment in Argentina, Brazil, and Mexico: Responding to the Debt Crisis**
John Williamson, ed./June 1983

3 **Inflation and Indexation: Argentina, Brazil, and Israel**
John Williamson, ed./March 1985

4 **Global Economic Imbalances**
C. Fred Bergsten, ed./December 1985

FORTHCOMING

Trade Policy for Troubled Industries
Gary Clyde Hufbauer and Howard F. Rosen

Domestic Adjustment and International Trade
Gary Clyde Hufbauer and Howard F. Rosen, eds.

Trade Protection in the United States: 31 Case Studies
Gary Clyde Hufbauer, Diane T. Berliner, and Kimberly Ann Elliott

Toward A New Development Strategy for Latin America
Bela Balassa, Gerardo M. Bueno, Pedro-Pablo Kucyznski, and Mario Henrique Simonsen

Another Multi-Fiber Arrangement?
William R. Cline

The Politics of Anti-Protection
I. M. Destler and John S. Odell

Japan in the World Economy
Bela Balassa and Marcus Noland

International Trade in Automobiles: Liberalization or Further Restraint?
William R. Cline

The Multiple Reserve Currency System
C. Fred Bergsten and John Williamson

Toward Cartelization of World Steel Trade?
William R. Cline

Trade Controls in Three Industries: The Automobile, Steel, and Textiles Cases
William R. Cline

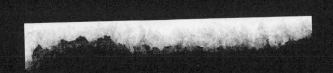

Lewis and Clark College - Watzek Library
HD73 .I43 1985b   wmain
/Global economic imbalances

3 5209 00343 5902